Frida Kahlo

Her Life in Paintings

SARA McINTOSH WOOTEN

Enslow Publishers, Inc.

40 Industrial Road   PO Box 38
Box 398   Aldershot
Berkeley Heights, NJ 07922   Hants GU12 6BP
USA   UK

http://www.enslow.com

Publisher's Note: This book includes photographs of some of Frida Kahlo's paintings. The captions give information about how the work was done, as well as the size of the painting. For instance, *oil on canvas* means Kahlo used oil paints on a piece of canvas. *8″ x 10½″* means the painting is 8 inches tall and 10½ inches wide.

Author's Note: Kahlo titled her paintings in Spanish, and their English translations sometimes vary. For example, *The Little Deer* may also be translated as *The Wounded Stag* or *The Little Stag*.

Library of Congress Cataloging-in-Publication Data

Wooten, Sara McIntosh.
    Frida Kahlo : her life in paintings / Sara McIntosh Wooten.— 1st ed.
        p. cm. — (Latino biography library)
    Includes bibliographical references and index.
    ISBN 0-7660-2487-3 (hardcover)
    1. Kahlo, Frida—Juvenile literature. 2. Painters—Mexico—Biography—Juvenile literature.
    I. Title. II. Series.
    ND259.K33W66 2005
    759.972—dc22

                                                                                        2004027539

Printed in the United States of America

10 9 8 7 6 5 4 3 2 1

To Our Readers:
We have done our best to make sure all Internet Addresses in this book were active and appropriate when we went to press. However, the author and the publisher have no control over and assume no liability for the material available on those Internet sites or on other Web sites they may link to. Any comments or suggestions can be sent by e-mail to comments@enslow.com or to the address on the back cover.

Every effort has been made to locate all copyright holders of material used in this book. If any errors or omissions have occurred, corrections will be made in future editions of this book.

Illustration Credits:
© **2005 Banco de México Diego Rivera & Frida Kahlo Museums Trust. Av. Cinco de Mayo No. 2, Col. Centro, Del. Cuauhtémoc 06059, México, D.F.:** Digital Images © Museum of Modern Art/Licensed by SCALA/Art Resource, NY, pp. 79, 81, 87. Instituto Nacional de Bellas Artes y Literatura, pp. 3, 33, 38. Photographs © Schalkwijk /Art Resource, NY, pp. 44, 57, 107.

AP/Wide World, pp. 15, 27, 92, 111, 112, 113; Archivo CENIDIAP-Instituto Nacional de Bellas Artes y Literatura, Mexico City, Mexico, pp. 11, 12, 18, 36, 41, 46, 49, 72, 106, 108; Associated Press, Detroit Institute of Arts, p. 64; Bárbara C. Cruz, p. 58; Christie's Images/Superstock, p. 74; Image is courtesy of the Florence Arquin papers, 1923–1985 in the Archives of American Art, Smithsonian Institution, p. 95; Library of Congress, p. 23; Library of Congress, Prints & Photographs Division, Carl Van Vechten Collection, p. 63; Photograph by Chester Dale. The image is courtesy of the Chester Dale papers, 1897–1971 (bulk 1950–1968) in the Archives of American Art, Smithsonian Institution, p. 100; Photograph by Florence Arquin. The image is courtesy of the Florence Arquin papers, 1923–1985 in the Archives of American Art, Smithsonian Institution, p. 102; Photographs by Nickolas Muray. © Nickolas Muray Photo Archives, Courtesy George Eastman House, pp. 1, 4, 8, 88; San Francisco Museum of Modern Art, Albert M. Bender Collection, Gift of Albert M. Bender, © Estate of Frida Kahlo, Courtesy Banco de Mexico, p. 55.

Cover Illustration: Photograph by Nickolas Muray. © Nickolas Muray Photo Archives, Courtesy George Eastman House.

Contents

Frida Kahlo

1

Tribute at Home

Police sirens wailed shortly after 8 P.M. as an ambulance, with police escort, carefully made its way through the crowd outside the Galería de Arte Contemporáneo (Gallery of Contemporary Art) in Mexico City, Mexico. It was April 13, 1953. The ambulance stopped outside the gallery, the doors to the vehicle opened, and the artist Frida Kahlo was carried inside on a stretcher.

At first glance, Kahlo did not look sick. She was dressed in colorful native Mexican dress. Heavy jewelry adorned her neck. Rings of different colors flashed from each of her fingers, and her carefully painted nails gleamed bright red. Her long black hair, braided and piled on her head, was interlaced with colorful ribbons that matched her outfit.

Yet despite her festive appearance that evening, Kahlo was desperately ill and heavily medicated against pain. At forty-five years of age, she had battled illness and pain since childhood. Most recently, a series of operations on her spine had resulted in a yearlong hospital stay. Even after that, her health had continued to decline, and she was frequently bedridden. Many people thought she would be too ill to attend the exhibit. Yet Kahlo ignored her doctor's warnings to stay home. She refused to miss her first solo exhibition in her beloved country of Mexico.

Inside the gallery, Kahlo was carefully placed on her four-poster canopied bed, which had been installed in the center of the room. Surrounding her were hundreds of friends, family, art critics, and well-wishers. Thirty-five of her paintings and drawings were on display.

The exhibition had been organized by Kahlo's friend Lola Alvarez Bravo, a photographer and the gallery's owner. She knew Kahlo was gravely ill and wanted to honor her life and work before she died.[1] Kahlo deeply appreciated Bravo's efforts and had eagerly looked forward to the event.[2] She had prepared handwritten invitations on heavy colored paper, tied with ribbons, beginning with the words:

> With friendship and affection
> straight from the heart,
> I have the pleasure to invite you
> to my humble exhibition.[3]

Once settled in her bed at the gallery, Kahlo greeted her guests as they gathered around to pay their respects. Those who had visited Kahlo at her home recognized the bed. A mirror attached inside the canopy allowed the bedridden artist to paint her self-portraits by simply looking up. Pictures of her friends, family, and political heroes covered the headboard, while papier-mâché skeletons danced from the bed's canopy.

> **"I am not sick. I am broken. But I am happy to be alive as long as I can paint."[4]**

Among the guests and well-wishers that evening was Kahlo's husband of almost twenty-five years, Diego Rivera. He was Mexico's most famous artist. At that time, Rivera's work was far more famous than Kahlo's. Yet Rivera, who had always admired his wife's work, was delighted with the success of the evening. Later, in his autobiography, he wrote, "For me, the most thrilling event of 1953 was Frida's one-man show in Mexico City. . . . Anyone who attended it could not but marvel at her great talent."[5]

As the guests viewed the exhibition, they came face-to-face with Kahlo's unusual style. Most of her work was of herself at various times in her life. Many paintings were quite small (12 inches by 18 inches) and conveyed her psychological or physical pain at the time they were painted. Kahlo often used a primitive, almost childlike style, as a way of incorporating and honoring Mexican folk art in her work. She also used symbols and elements from Mexican history to convey her message.

Among the paintings on display was *The Little Deer*, which she had completed in 1946. In this painting,

Kahlo's pet deer Granizo modeled for her painting *The Little Deer*.

Kahlo portrayed herself as a deer bounding through the forest. Arrows pierce the animal's body and the wounds drip blood. Looking out from under the antlers is not the face of a deer—it is Kahlo. The deer, like Kahlo, is surely suffering, but the expression on the face does not show her pain.

Another painting, set off a bit from the other works of art, was *Tree of Hope*, also completed in 1946. This painting is divided vertically into a day side and a night side. Kahlo appears twice in the painting. The day side shows her lying on a hospital bed with her back exposed to the viewer. The surgical incisions from a recent operation are clearly visible. In the night side of the painting, Kahlo wears traditional Mexican dress and seems to be watching over her hospital self. In her hand she holds a medical corset, along with a flag bearing the words TREE OF HOPE, KEEP FIRM. She is crying, yet determined. The painting projects her as a victim as well as a survivor.

The exhibition was a triumph for Kahlo. Many more guests attended than were expected, and the exhibit would stay open for a month to allow for the steady stream of people who wanted to see her work. As the evening drew to a close, guests gathered around Kahlo's bed and sang her favorite Mexican songs until after midnight.

The great evening honoring Frida Kahlo finally ended. Despite her illness, everyone there that night had experienced Kahlo's enduring spirit as seen in her art, her fiery determination and love of drama, and her devotion to Mexico and its people.

2

A Difficult Start

Magdalena Carmen Frida Kahlo y Calderón was born on a rainy July 6, 1907, at her home in Coyoacán, Mexico. Located about an hour southwest of Mexico City, Coyoacán was a small village at that time. Frida had two older sisters, Matilde and Adriana. The youngest child in the family, Cristina, was born just ten months after Frida.

Frida's mother, Matilde Calderón, was of Spanish and Mexican Indian descent. A strict parent and devout Catholic, Matilde made sure that her children were brought up in the Catholic faith. They went to church every day and faithfully gave a prayer of thanks before each meal.

Matilde was also a diligent housekeeper. She fulfilled her duty to teach her daughters how to cook, take care of the house, sew, and embroider. In those days, few women had careers outside their homes. Most young

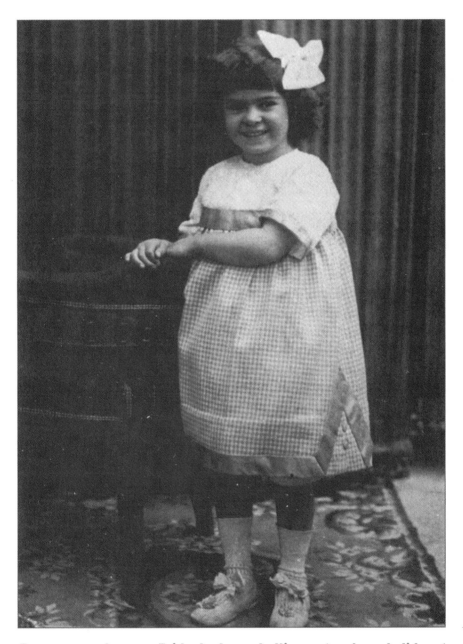

From an early age, Frida had a rebellious streak and did not always follow the rules.

Frida's mother, Matilde Calderón.

girls in Mexico went on to marry, raise children, and take care of their families.

Frida and Cristina rebelled against their mother's rules for the household. Behind her back the girls called her "Mi Jefe" ("My Chief.") They also failed to view their religious training with the reverence Matilde expected. When all the others had their eyes closed during mealtime prayers, the two girls would secretly exchange glances and suppress giggles. Frida respected her mother but was not especially close to her during childhood.[1]

Frida's father had been born in Germany. His parents, who were Jewish, settled there after moving from Hungary. His name was Wilhelm. By the time he was nineteen, Wilhelm had developed epilepsy, a brain disorder that causes seizures. The seizures became so disruptive that he quit his studies at the University of Nuremberg. Instead, he decided to leave home and start a new life in Mexico. Once there, he changed his first name to Guillermo, which is Spanish for William.

At first, unable to speak Spanish, Guillermo took a series of jobs with other German immigrants. Over time, he learned the Spanish language. In 1894 he married, but his wife died four years later during the birth of their second daughter. Soon afterward he met and married Matilde Calderón, another employee at the jewelry store where he was working. Matilde refused to allow Guillermo's two daughters to live with them; instead, they were sent to a convent.

Matilde's father, a photographer, encouraged his new son-in-law to come work in his studio. Guillermo's career as a photographer began to flourish. In 1904 he was chosen by the Mexican government to photograph historic buildings and archaeological sites in Mexico.

With the money he made from his government photography, Guillermo was able to buy land and build a home on the corner of Allende and Londres Streets, just two blocks from the town plaza in Coyoacán. The Kahlo home would hold a central place in Frida's life. She was born there, lived there for many of her adult years, and would ultimately die there.

The home, made of thick, white stucco walls with a flat roof, was built in a U shape, with the rooms opening onto a private courtyard in the middle. While the building was originally white, it was later painted a deep, vivid blue and became known as La Casa Azul, or the Blue House. The courtyard was filled with lush tropical plants and a variety of flowers and fruit trees. Frida and her family spent many hours there enjoying the tranquillity.

Frida's father was a quiet, private man. His photography studio was in Mexico City, so he left home early in the mornings, returning each evening about eight.

Tired from the day, he would retreat to the parlor and play classical music on the family piano for a while. After that, his wife would serve him dinner, which he ate alone and in silence.

In 1910, life throughout Mexico was interrupted by revolution. It was the country's hundredth anniversary of its independence from Spain. Yet many people in the country were unhappy and oppressed by the thirty-four-year reign of General Porfirio Diáz, the president who ruled as a dictator.

The vast majority of Mexico's people under Diáz's rule were very poor, living in shacks, slums, or on the streets. Most did not have access to sewage systems or running water. Diseases took their toll among the poor. In addition, most people could not read or write, and little work was available to them. The few opportunities for unskilled workers paid next to nothing. Diáz had encouraged foreign countries to take over much of Mexico's industry and land, which infuriated Mexican people of all classes.

In response to these conditions, peasants and farmers rebelled in 1910. Led by such revolutionaries as Francisco "Pancho" Villa and Emiliano Zapata, they took up arms against the Diáz government. At times, Frida could hear the sound of gunfire outside her home in Coyoacán. She later recalled that her mother fed hungry rebel soldiers.[2]

By 1912, General Diáz had been overthrown. He was no longer in power, but Mexico's problems were far

Many Mexicans fought to overthrow the dictator Porfirio Diaz and his government. Frida identified closely with the spirit of the revolution.

from over. Many more years of infighting among various factions would take place before a stable government was established under the leadership of Alvaro Obregón, who became president in 1920.

With all the government upheaval, Guillermo's job as official photographer for Mexico ended. After that, he continued to work as a photographer, but his income was greatly reduced. The family fell on hard times, which would continue throughout Guillermo's lifetime.

In 1913, when Frida was six, she was stricken with polio. The disease began with intense pain in her right leg. Polio, which is caused by a virus, can result in permanently weakened leg muscles or paralysis. It can disable its victims for life. In the early 1950s, a vaccine was developed to prevent polio, but when Frida was a girl, there was no cure for it. She had to stay in bed for nine months while she recovered from her illness. Once she had recuperated, her right leg was shorter and thinner than the left one.

To occupy herself during endless hours in bed, Frida would blow on a window in her room, then use her finger to draw a door on the condensation that formed. After that, her imagination would take over. In her mind's eye she flew through the "door" and crossed a field that lay beyond it, finally arriving at a local dairy owned by the Pinzón family. Spiriting herself through the O in the store's sign, she descended to the earth's core, "where my imaginary friend always waited for me. I don't remember her appearance or her color," Frida later wrote. "But I do remember her joyfulness—she laughed a lot. She was agile, and danced as if she were weightless."[3] When Frida grew tired of playing with her magical friend, she would return to her room in the way she had left. She completed her journey by rubbing out the door she had drawn.

Frida was slender and well coordinated despite her shortened leg. As she grew stronger after her illness, her father encouraged her to strengthen her right leg by playing different kinds of sports. She participated in soccer, bicycling, swimming, and wrestling. These were unusual activities for a young girl at that time, and Frida was considered a tomboy.

Frida was enrolled in a German elementary school, the Colegio Alemán. She started school late because of her extended illness, so she was older than other students in her grade. To keep from drawing unwanted attention to herself, Frida told her classmates that she was younger than she really was. As she grew older, she continued the lie, saying that she was born in 1910. She chose that year in honor of the beginning of the Mexican Revolution. She wanted to identify herself with that event and bind herself to her country's history.[4]

> "My imaginary friend . . . laughed a lot. She was agile, and danced as if she were weightless."

Frida's schoolmates ridiculed her misshapen leg. They tormented her, shouting, *"Frida, pata de palo!"* ("Frida, peg leg!") The teasing hurt her feelings.[5] To compensate, she learned to show off by doing special stunts on her bicycle and skates.[6] She also wore extra socks on her right leg to make it look thicker, along with a shoe with a higher heel so she would not limp.

Frida and her father were especially close as she grew up; she was his favorite among his daughters.[7] He thought her personality was much like his. Guillermo also considered Frida to be the most intelligent of his children.[8] On weekends Frida would sometimes go with her father on photography jobs. He taught her how to use his cameras, develop photographs, and hand color the images. (Although color photography was invented

Frida's father did not show his love openly, but Frida was clearly his favorite child. He taught her about nature and photography.

in 1904, it did not become practical enough for widespread use until 1935.)

As she grew older, Frida helped her father carry his camera equipment. She also knew what to do if he should have an epilepsy attack. She later wrote, "I learned how to help him during his attacks in the middle of the street. . . . I kept watch so that nobody would steal his photographic equipment."[9]

Guillermo shared his love of nature with his daughter. Using his books for references, the two took field trips together to nearby parks and into the surrounding countryside. They liked to observe the animals, plants, birds, and insects. Sometimes Frida brought specimens home to look at under her father's microscope.

Guillermo enjoyed painting as a hobby and introduced Frida to that as well. He helped her experiment with sketching and sometimes let her use his paints and brushes. She later wrote, "My childhood was wonderful even though my father was a sick man. He was the best example for me of tenderness and workmanship, but above all of understanding for all my problems."[10]

As Frida grew up, she also enjoyed exploring Coyoacán with her friends and her sisters. She especially liked visiting the street vendors who sold their wares in open booths in the town plaza near her home. There she could buy little toys for a few *pesos*, or sample tempting foods cooked on the spot, such as quesadillas (corn tortillas filled with melted cheese, onions, and hot peppers).

Despite her bout with polio, Frida grew into a confident young woman. The days ahead shone brightly.

3

Changed Forever

In 1922, when Frida was fifteen years old, she began high school at the National Preparatory School in Mexico City. Nicknamed La Prepa, it was the finest high school in Mexico.[1] Frida's mother did not think her daughter should attend. After all, what need would a girl have for a challenging education? But when Frida made high scores on the entrance examinations, Guillermo insisted that she enroll. He wanted her to make the most of her intelligence and abilities.[2]

Academically, La Prepa was considered Mexico's toughest high school. The professors were well known in their fields. The students who attended were among the best and brightest of Mexico's youth. Most were preparing themselves for the National University. When Frida began at La Prepa, the school had just recently started admitting female students. In 1922, she was one of only thirty-five girls out of the school's two thousand students.

The high school was an hour away from Frida's home in Coyoacán, and she rode a trolley to get there each day. Located near the heart of Mexico City, the school was surrounded by shops and open markets, government buildings, the National Palace, and the National Cathedral.

By this time, Frida had become an attractive young woman. She was petite and slender, with thick black hair. Her intense brown eyes slanted up just a bit, and the trace of a mustache graced her upper lip. Her striking appearance was further set off by dark, full eyebrows, which met in the middle of her forehead. Frida never tried to lessen the effect of her eyebrows. They became part of her look, reminding some of a black bird with wings spread in flight.[3]

Frida began her high school career at La Prepa dressed like a proper German schoolgirl. She wore a navy pleated skirt, white blouse, necktie, knee socks, and a straw hat with long ribbons trailing down the back. That disciplined, schoolgirl look would not last, however. Before long she started showing her independence and individuality by wearing overalls and pants to her classes, which was very unusual for a girl at that time.

Frida's individuality was also reflected in her career interest. She wanted to become a doctor. While women doctors abound today, in 1922 the goal was considered bold and rather odd for a young girl.

Frida was ready for the academic challenges of La Prepa. She learned to read in three languages: Spanish, German, and English. Without much effort she was able to keep excellent grades throughout her years there. Even so, she was not a model student. She began to skip the classes she thought were boring, preferring to explore the streets of Mexico City instead.[4] She also picked up rough language from the streets and enjoyed using it. It was a practice considered shocking and in very bad taste for a girl.[5] The teasing and suffering she had endured as a child had toughened Frida into a fiercely independent, strong-willed young woman who did not worry about others' opinions.[6]

In class Frida found it amusing to draw unflattering sketches of her professors, which were secretly passed around during lectures. At one point, she was expelled from La Prepa, but she convincingly pleaded her case to the minister of education. He let her back in, while scolding the school principal for being unable to keep his student's behavior under control.[7]

Because of her family's financial difficulties, Frida worked at a variety of jobs after school and during school breaks. She was a cashier at a pharmacy for a while, and later kept accounting books for a lumber-yard. After that, her father got her a job as an assistant to a commercial printer, Fernando Fernández, who was a friend of his. Fernández quickly recognized Frida's

Frida liked to buy little trinkets and tasty treats from the street vendors in Mexico City.

artistic ability.[8] He encouraged her to draw and gave her assignments copying prints to improve her skill.

As at any school, the students at La Prepa formed groups, or cliques, depending upon their interests. Frida identified with a group called the Cachuchas. It was a small union of seven boys and two girls. They were named for the red crocheted caps they all wore.

The Cachuchas were a spirited group—intelligent and mischievous. They met regularly at the Ibero-American Library, a few blocks from La Prepa. There they discussed the latest books they had read. They competed to see who could discover the most interesting books and finish reading them first. In addition to literature, the group also enjoyed discussing art, history, and philosophy.

The Cachuchas debated Mexican politics as well. They sympathized with the problems of the under-privileged and working classes in Mexico and around the world. Fiercely proud of their Mexican heritage, the group had high hopes for their country's future.[9] All fine students, each of the Cachuchas would have distinguished careers as adults. Most remained life-long friends with Frida.

Despite their intelligence and quest for knowledge, the Cachuchas had nothing but contempt for the school's administration and rules. They delighted in creating mischief and were responsible for a parade of pranks at La Prepa. Once they set off firecrackers in class to enliven a boring lecture. Another time they sent a donkey wandering through the school's hallways.

With their close contact and similar interests, it was not long before Frida fell in love with the leader of the Cachuchas, Alejandro Gómez Arias. Handsome, intelligent, and charismatic, Alejandro was three years older than Frida. He returned her affection, and the two became a couple.

Alejandro's well-to-do family did not think Frida, with her outlandish ways, was an acceptable girlfriend for their son. She was not allowed to visit him at his home. In those days it was not considered proper for a girl and boy to spend time together alone. But Frida was not concerned with what other people thought. She aggressively pursued her relationship with Alejandro, sneaking around to be alone with him. They met secretly in the city, with Frida making up excuses to tell her mother where she was going.

When they could not see each other, Frida and Alejandro wrote letters. Her letters were filled with news about what was going on at home, and they often included little sketches to accompany her words. She was not shy about expressing her love for Alejandro, signing one letter: "You know I adore you."[10]

During her years at La Prepa, Frida did not have many female friends. She thought most girls were silly and petty.[11] In turn, most of the young women at La Prepa did not approve of Frida's behavior. They thought she was too wild.[12] Still, Frida felt no need to change her unconventional ways. She once wrote to Alejandro, "The fact is that now no one wants to be my friend because I have lost my reputation, something that I cannot remedy. I will have to be friends with those who like me the way I am."[13]

As the new government of Alvaro Obregón took hold in Mexico in 1920, changes of all sorts were in store for the country. Modernizing Mexico and redistributing land to give opportunities to the poor became top priorities. The Obregón government also supported labor unions in their fight for fair wages. In addition, José Vasconcelos, the new minister of education, began a broad program to promote education for the masses of illiterate Mexicans. He also wanted to encourage appreciation for native Mexican heritage, culture, and crafts.

As part of his plan, in 1922 Vasconcelos commissioned

A new spirit of pride in native Mexican culture and heritage took hold among Mexicans after a stable government was established in 1920. This new sense of patriotism was called Mexicanidad.[14] Mexican mural art, such as the work of Diego Rivera, one of Mexico's most prominent artists, was an important way of expressing this patriotism.

the artist Diego Rivera to paint a mural in the auditorium at La Prepa. The idea was that art should be enjoyed by all the Mexican people, not just those rich enough to visit museums. Vasconcelos wanted large murals created in public places showing the glory of Mexico's vast history and culture. They would help the Mexican people learn about, and be proud of, their heritage.

The mural Rivera would create was entitled *Creation*. The massive wall he was asked to paint covered a space of 150 square feet. To prepare, worktables were set up for mixing paints and plaster. Scaffolding (a system of ladders and platforms) was constructed so that Rivera could reach the heights of his work space. He first sketched his concept for the mural on a grid. Then he recreated the grid on the wall, sketching the scenes in charcoal. Once that stage was completed, he began painting.

Rivera was a striking man in appearance. Six feet tall, he weighed well over three hundred pounds, with a big potbelly and protruding eyes. Not a fancy dresser,

While Rivera was busy painting from a wooden scaffold, the schoolgirl Frida enjoyed watching him and pulling pranks.

he usually sported a cowboy hat; heavy miner's work shoes; baggy, wrinkled clothing that was often dirty; and a wide leather belt. Still, with his fame as an artist, his intellectual wit, and his charismatic personality, women were drawn to him.

Students were not allowed in the auditorium while Rivera, or "El Maestro" (the Master), as he was called, was working. That did not stop Frida. She was intent on seeing the great artist at work. She would sneak into the auditorium and watch him for hours at a time. As Rivera later recorded in his autobiography, "[Frida] was dressed like any other high school student, but her manner immediately set her apart. She had unusual dignity and self-assurance, and there was a strange fire in her eyes."[15]

Frida's mischievous nature kicked in as well. She took great delight in teasing the artist, calling him *Panzón* (fat belly) and giving him false alerts that his wife or one of his girlfriends was approaching. Sometimes she stole food from his lunch basket. Once, she soaped the auditorium steps, imagining the hilarity of watching Rivera slip and fall. Thwarting her plan, Rivera maneuvered the steps with ease. The next day, however, Frida's efforts were rewarded when one of her most detested teachers, Professor Antonio Case, took the fall instead.

Frida Kahlo's life held all the promise a young Mexican woman could hope for. She was intelligent and creative, with a bright future ahead. But on September 17, 1925, her life changed forever. She and Alejandro met in the city that day to spend time together. As the afternoon wore on, they boarded a crowded wooden bus to return to Coyoacán, finding seats near the back. Then disaster struck. The bus passed in front of an electric trolley just as the trolley was turning, and Frida's bus was hit. Unable to stop, the trolley continued to press into

> *Rivera liked Frida's "unusual dignity and self-assurance, and there was a strange fire in her eyes."*

the bus, finally pushing it into a wall. With nowhere to go, the bus exploded from the trolley's pressure. The passengers were thrown out, with many falling under the trolley.

Alejandro landed under the bus but escaped with only cuts and bruises. Frida's fate was quite different. She lay on the ground with the bus's metal handrail protruding from her pelvis. Her clothes had been blown off by the force of the collision, and her body was covered with blood. One of the passengers had been carrying a bag of gold dust, probably for use in painting, which had torn open during the crash. The gold dust rained down, coating her body.

Frida remained conscious and in shock, worrying about a little toy she had bought that afternoon.[16] Then a passerby braced his knee against Frida's body and pulled the handrail out. The sound of her screams could be heard over the wail of the ambulance siren as it approached the wreck. She was carried to a nearby pool hall, her broken body placed on a pool table and covered with Alejandro's torn coat. Together they waited for help to arrive. Frida was taken to the Red Cross Hospital, a charity hospital that served the poor. There, doctors assessed the extent of her injuries. They found that her spine was broken in three places, along with her collarbone and two ribs. Her right leg had eleven fractures; her right foot was dislocated and crushed. Her left shoulder had been pulled out of joint, and her pelvis was broken in three places. Frida had so many injuries that the doctors did not expect her to live.

4

Beginning Again

Alejandro Arias knew that Frida's life had changed forever. He later wrote, "A new Frida started to die and to live."[1]

When Frida's parents were told of the accident and her condition, they fell apart. Guillermo immediately became ill, which prevented him from visiting Frida for three weeks. Matilde was so upset that she did not speak for a month. She was never able to gather the strength to visit her daughter in the hospital.[2] Frida's parents were in shock, certain their daughter would die. They could not bring themselves to talk about it with anyone, even family members. Frida's older sister Matilde read about the accident in a newspaper and immediately went to see her. She continued to visit Frida regularly and did her best to raise her sister's spirits. Matilde helped pass the time by entertaining Frida with jokes.

The Red Cross Hospital had originally been built as a convent. By the time Frida was a patient there, it was old, dark, and worn down. Frida was placed in a large ward along with twenty-four other patients. With only one nurse assigned to the ward, Frida did not get a lot of attention. She reported that the food there was terrible.[3] On top of that, her body was encased in a plaster cast with a wooden frame so that her extensive injuries could heal. Her head was the only part of her body that she could move.

In mid-October, Frida was released from the hospital and sent home. Despite her dreadful experience there, she had mixed feelings when it was time to go home. She could not wait to get out of the hospital; yet she dreaded the coming weeks in bed without daily contact from her school friends.[4]

Once back at home, Frida had to stay in bed for the next two months. Her body was still in a plaster cast that reached from her neck to her hips. In a letter to Alejandro in December, she told him of her frustration: "The only good thing is that I'm starting to get used to suffering."[5]

Because of her injuries, Frida missed the fall semester at La Prepa, and she never returned to school. To her delight, some of her school friends came to visit her in Coyoacán, which gave her a break from the loneliness and boredom at home. With her friends, she presented a brave front. She laughed and entertained them, keeping her pain private and not complaining. As one friend

A year after the accident, Frida made this sketch. Pencil on paper. 8″ x 10½″.

later recalled, "When we went to visit her when she was sick, she played, she laughed, she commented, she made caustic criticisms, witticisms, and wise opinions. If she cried, no one knew it."[6]

With Alejandro, however, Frida was more open about her pain. She continued writing letters to him as she recovered, frankly describing the anguish and frustration of her condition. She wrote, "You can't imagine how it hurts; every time they pull me I cry a liter of tears. . . . My leg hurts so very much, one must think that it is crushed."[7] Alejandro visited her occasionally, but never enough to satisfy her need for his attention.[8]

As a distraction from her pain and boredom, Frida decided to take up painting, even though she had practically no training in art. Her only formal experience had been from the two required art classes she had taken in high school, along with her work copying drawings for her job at the print shop. But she had always liked to sketch, and she had filled notebooks with drawings in her spare time. She also often added illustrations to her letters.

Frida's mother hired a carpenter to build an easel that she could use lying down in bed. Matilde also installed a mirror on the underside of the bed canopy, so that Frida could see herself as she painted. Alejandro would later reflect, "[Frida's] hands were not destroyed, that and her forced immobility determined her destiny, painting."[9]

By December 1925, Frida was walking well enough

to return to work. Yet the accident would remain with her for the rest of her life. She would be reminded of it each day with the ever-present pain she felt, especially in her back and in her right leg.

> *"The only good thing is that I'm starting to get used to suffering."*

In 1926, the Kahlos posed for a formal family portrait. In the photograph, Frida's independent spirit is clear. Her hair is parted in the middle and pulled tightly back in a severe style for a girl. She wears a man's suit, complete with vest, necktie, and handkerchief. One hand rests lightly on a man's walking cane. Her defiant attitude comes through as she stares directly at the camera without the hint of a smile.

At the end of the summer, Frida, age nineteen, was back in bed again. This time she had to wear a plaster corset (a stiff body brace that extended from her chest to her hips) to help relieve the severe pain in her back. At the same time, she realized that Alejandro was beginning to drift away from her emotionally. In an attempt to regain his attention, she began to paint her first self-portrait. She completed it in the fall and gave it to him.

The portrait presents an elegant Frida, in a formal pose and wearing a dark red velvet dress. The dark background gives the painting a sad quality. She sits with her right hand open, suggesting her hope that they

Frida's father took this family portrait in 1926. *Standing:* Frida, in men's clothing. *Back row:* her aunt, her aunt's sister Adriana, and Adriana's husband Alberto Veraza. *Middle row:* her uncle, her mother, her cousin Carmen. Front row: Carlos Veraza, Cristina.

might get back together again.[10] Even though it was her first serious work, Frida's talent as an artist was clear.[11]

The portrait touched Alejandro's heart, and the two renewed their relationship for a time. But in March 1927, his parents sent him on a six-month vacation to Europe. They hoped that a separation would cool his feelings for Frida and that he would move on with his life.

Frida was devastated by Alejandro's departure.[12] She clung to the hope that their romance would survive despite his absence. But that part of her relationship with Alejandro was over. Even so, they would remain friends for the rest of her life.

In the meantime, Frida's physical pain only continued, as did her discouragement with her condition. Frida was still trapped in a plaster body cast. It had to be changed from time to time. Whenever she needed a new one, she was suspended upright with only the tips of her toes touching the floor while the plaster was applied to her body. She had to remain in that position for several hours until the plaster dried.[13]

The pain never stopped. In May 1927, she wrote, "The pain continues exactly the same in my bad leg and sometimes the good one hurts too; so I'm getting worse and worse, and without the least hope of getting better."[14] Yet Frida continued to paint, creating portraits of her friend Alicia Galant in 1927 and of her sister Cristina the following year, among others.

In the fall of 1927, Frida had a second operation.

Frida painted her first self-portrait as a gift for her high school boyfriend. 1926. Oil on canvas. 31″ x 23″.

This one was to mend three vertebrae in her spine. It was an injury from the bus accident that had not been recognized or treated at the time. Once again she found herself immobilized in a body cast for months.

By 1928, Kahlo was spending time with a new group of friends. They included a variety of intellectuals, writers, artists, and political activists with similar interests and concerns. Among them was a woman named Tina Modotti, an Italian-born photographer. Tina, along with many of Frida's other new friends, was a member of Mexico's Communist Party. Frida also joined the party in 1928.

Communism is built upon an economic theory first proposed by Karl Marx and Friedrich Engels in their book *Communist Manifesto*, written in 1848. The book outlines the idea for a system in which a country's resources and industries are owned by the community, rather than by individuals. In a Communist economy,

The theories proposed by Marx and Engels did not have much influence during their lifetime. But their ideas were revised and developed in the twentieth century by Russian Vladimir Ilich Lenin. He successfully led the Russian people in a revolution against their government in 1917. Lenin's new system of government, based on the fundamentals outlined in the *Communist Manifesto*, came to be known as Communism.

the idea is that everyone works for the good of all. At the same time, everyone's needs are met by the community. In theory, this kind of system would eliminate the vast differences in wealth among individuals. Marx and Engels went so far as to encourage workers and peasants to rise up in violent revolt against their bosses in order to set up this way of life.

Capitalism is the economic opposite of Communism. Under capitalism, the economic system in the United States, businesses are owned by individuals, not by the government. Private companies make products and offer services to make a profit. With capitalism, the more enterprising and efficient businesses will make more money.

Frida and her Communist friends believed that Communism was the only kind of government that could raise living standards for poor, uneducated, and disadvantaged people, not only in Mexico but around the world. In contrast, they saw the capitalist system of the United States as an evil and uncaring system that allowed the rich to get richer while the poor remained in hopeless poverty.

Tina Modotti often held parties at her apartment, where her friends would discuss their political views. At one of Modotti's parties in 1928, Frida came in contact with another Communist of earlier acquaintance: the famous Mexican muralist Diego Rivera. This time, their meeting would have far-reaching effects for both of them.

For this picture, Frida crossed her legs so the right one would not appear smaller.

Rivera was born in 1886 in Guanajuato, Mexico. At twenty, he moved to Europe, where he studied art in Spain and France for the next fourteen years. During his stay in Europe, Rivera met and became friends with the Spanish painter Pablo Picasso. Rivera experimented with cubism, a style of painting developed by Picasso. With cubism, figures are presented as geometric fragments. After a number of years, however, Rivera became tired of cubism. He wanted to paint in a more natural style. He also wanted to go back to Mexico and create paintings that could be seen and appreciated by all people, not just the museumgoers.[15]

Rivera was known for his larger-than-life personality. He entertained his friends with exaggerated or completely made-up stories about his life. He was notorious for his relationships with attractive women. Throughout his adult life, Rivera had many love affairs. By the time he met Kahlo, he had been married once and had also lived in a long-term common-law marriage with another woman.

Despite his flaws, Rivera had a reputation as a tireless worker. He became completely absorbed in his projects and often painted throughout the night. Like many Mexican men of the time, the hot-tempered Rivera usually carried a pistol as protection.

Soon after crossing paths again with Rivera, Frida decided to take some of her paintings to show him. She respected his talent as an artist, and wanted to ask his opinion of her work. She thought he could tell her if she had enough talent to seriously pursue painting as an occupation. Rivera was high up on his scaffold, painting, when he heard a voice calling out to him.

Rivera later called that meeting "one of the happiest events in my life. I heard a young girl shouting up to me, 'Diego, please come down from there! I have something important to discuss with you!'"[16] Kahlo showed Rivera three of her portraits. "As I looked at them, one by one," Rivera continued, "I was immediately impressed. It was obvious to me that this girl was an authentic artist."[17]

Rivera asked to see more of Kahlo's work. He promised to stop by her home the next Sunday afternoon to look at it. That visit led to more, and their romance began. Rivera was forty-one; Kahlo was twenty-one.

In the meantime, Rivera had finished the mural at La Prepa and was working on a new one at Mexico's Ministry of Education building. Entitled *The Ballad of the Proletarian Revolution*, it was a huge project that would consume several years of Rivera's life.

As their relationship developed, Kahlo often visited Rivera while he was working at the Ministry of Education. He used her as a model in one panel, titled *Insurrection*. She is shown dressed in a red shirt, handing out rifles and bayonets to workers and peasants as they prepare for revolution.

Kahlo's father was concerned about his daughter's budding romance. He saw Rivera as a bad match, considering the vast difference in their ages along with

In this detail of Rivera's mural, Kahlo is pictured in the center, with short hair, giving weapons to the revolutionaries.

Rivera's reputation as a womanizer. Kahlo's mother was even more displeased. She thought Rivera was too old and too fat for Frida. She also found fault because he was a Communist and—even worse—an atheist.[18] Kahlo's friends were equally shocked at their relationship, calling it "una cosa monstruosa" ("a hideous thing").[19] Because of the striking differences in their looks, Frida said they had been called the "elephant and the dove."[20]

Kahlo continued painting portraits through 1928 and 1929, and she received enthusiastic encouragement from Rivera. Yet he did not teach her or try to influence her style.[21] She developed her own, which was unique. At first, because of her inexperience, she painted in a primitive, childlike way. Her subjects looked stiff. Backgrounds and objects often seemed distorted and unrealistic.[22] Later, as she became more skilled, Kahlo would intentionally create that primitive effect. She wanted to replicate and honor the style of Mexican folk art paintings, which were created by untrained artists.[23]

Along with her painting, Rivera and Kahlo's relationship continued to flourish. By the summer of 1929, they began planning to marry.

The wedding portrait: Kahlo and Rivera were married in 1929.

5

Life in Love

Kahlo had never been one to follow orders, and she ignored her parents' objections to her relationship with Rivera. In addition to being in love with him, her decision to marry Rivera had a practical side. By this time she was the last unmarried daughter in the Kahlo household. Her parents were still having difficulty making ends meet financially, and their problems grew worse with her continual medical expenses. Rivera, although far from perfect, was famous, wealthy, and known for his generous spirit. By marrying him, Kahlo would have financial security.

Kahlo and Rivera were married in a civil ceremony by the Coyoacán mayor at the town's city hall on August 21, 1929. Her father attended the wedding; her mother did not. Because of Rivera's fame, the wedding made the society column in newspapers not only in Mexico but throughout the United States and Europe.

After the ceremony, Tina Modotti hosted a big party for the newlyweds at her apartment. The evening began well; food was plentiful and a mariachi band (a Mexican band with violins, trumpets, and guitars) provided festive music. However, as the night wore on, problems developed. Rivera, having had too much alcohol to drink, began firing his pistol. In the chaos that followed, one guest's finger was broken, and some of Modotti's furniture was damaged. In addition, Rivera's former wife, Lupe Marín, attended the party. She grew jealous seeing Rivera with his new wife. In a rage, she created an unpleasant scene by insulting Kahlo and making fun of her deformed right leg. Finally, Rivera and Kahlo got into an argument. Kahlo left in tears to return to her home in Coyoacán. It was several days before their tempers cooled. Then Rivera fetched his bride and took her to his home at 104 Paseo de la Reforma.

Soon after their marriage, Kahlo began to dress in the style she would become known for. At her husband's suggestion, she began to wear the colorful native costume worn by the women of the Isthmus of Tehuantepec in southern Mexico. Rivera had spent time there in 1921, immersing himself in Mexican culture as he prepared to paint the La Prepa mural. He had been impressed with the Tehuana women and their legendary beauty, intelligence, and independence.

Kahlo loved dressing like a Tehuana woman. It made her feel connected to her native Mexican heritage.[1] Each day she took great care in choosing her outfit.[2]

Rivera loved to see Kahlo dressed in the traditional Tehuana style.

She wore a long, full skirt over white petticoats, a brightly embroidered blouse, and *huaraches* (leather sandals). She also usually added a shawl, called a *rebozo*. The long skirts were colorful and eye-catching. They also hid Kahlo's deformed leg, along with the scars from surgery. Kahlo accented her outfits with lots of heavy, pre-Columbian Mexican jewelry—gold or silver necklaces, bracelets, and rings with native jade or obsidian stones. Kahlo loved jewelry, and over the years her husband would give her many pieces to go with her outfits.[3]

During the first few months of their marriage, Kahlo did not paint very much. She devoted herself to her husband, going with him each day to his work site to watch him paint. In turn, Rivera valued his wife's opinion of his work.[4]

Shortly after their marriage, the United States Ambassador to Mexico, Dwight W. Morrow, invited Rivera and Kahlo to dinner at his home in Cuernavaca. Morrow was aware of Rivera's fame and success as a muralist. He asked Rivera to paint a series of murals at the Cortés Palace in Cuernavaca. It had been built in 1530 by Hernán Cortés. The murals were to be a gift to the people of Mexico from the United States. They would show the history of the conquest of Mexico. With Cuernavaca about a ninety-minute distance from Mexico City and the Morrows out of the country for most of the year, Morrow offered Kahlo and Rivera the use of their home. There, Rivera would be close to his work.

As the days wore on, the newlyweds settled into their

new life together. Kahlo enjoyed her role as Rivera's attentive wife. She liked cooking for her husband and taking care of the Morrows' home. Every day Rivera went to work on his mural. She would often take him lunch in a basket decorated with flowers, just as Mexican peasant women took lunch to their husbands while they worked in the fields.

The couple developed pet names for each other as well. She called him *Sapo-Rana* (Toad-Frog) or *Cara de Sapo* (Frog Face). He referred to her as his *Chiquita* (Little One). They appreciated each other and the qualities and interests they had in common—their intelligence, political views, and love of art.

Although Rivera's fame as a muralist had brought him much success and admiration, his work was not approved of by the Communist Party. High-ranking party officials did not think it was fitting that he painted for the Mexican government. They did not like some of his friends, either, or the fact that he argued at party meetings. In 1929 Rivera was expelled from the Communist Party. He was very hurt by the action, saying, "I did not have a home—the Party having always been my home."[5] To show support for her husband, Kahlo resigned from the party as well.

Because of his work on the mammoth Ministry of Education murals, Rivera's fame had spread. By the fall of 1930, he had another invitation to paint a mural—this time in the United States. Rivera had difficulty getting a visa to enter the United States because of his well-known Communist beliefs and former party membership. But with help from a friend in the United States, he finally got approval, and he and Kahlo went to San Francisco. There he would paint a mural in the Luncheon Club of the Pacific Stock Exchange building. In addition, he got a commission to paint a smaller work at the California School of Fine Arts (now called the San Francisco Art Institute).

Rivera was delighted at the chance to work in the United States.[6] Kahlo had also long been interested in traveling there.[7] The couple would be abroad for six months.

Once in San Francisco, Rivera and Kahlo were welcomed with parties, lavish dinners, and receptions. Their visit was covered by the press. Rivera was viewed as a celebrity, and doors were opened to him. He met San Francisco's most prominent citizens, business leaders, and art enthusiasts.

With her striking looks and clothing, Kahlo also caught the attention of the people of San Francisco. She was not seen as just the wife of a famous artist. Photographer Edward Weston met Rivera and Kahlo while they were in San Francisco and later recorded his impressions. "I photographed Diego again, his new wife—Frieda—too. . . . She is a little doll alongside Diego, but a doll in size only, for she is strong and quite beautiful. . . . Dressed in native costume even to huaraches, she causes much excitement on the streets of San Francisco. People stop in their tracks to look in wonder," Weston wrote.[8] He noticed that the people of San Francisco were fascinated by this petite, exotic Mexican beauty.

As for Kahlo, she liked San Francisco very much.[9] She enjoyed exploring the city, which occupied her time while Rivera was at work each day. She was also determined to improve her English, which she found to be a challenge.[10]

On the other hand, Kahlo was less impressed with the American people. She wrote, "I don't like gringos [non-Hispanics] that much; they are very dull people and they all have faces that look like uncooked bread."[11]

Before long, Kahlo began to complain of pain in her right foot, which made it hard for her to walk. She was admitted to San Francisco General Hospital as a patient of Dr. Leo Eloesser. He was a friend of Rivera's and a highly respected bone surgeon. Dr. Eloesser diagnosed her with scoliosis, a spinal deformity that can cause severe nerve damage over time.

Kahlo and her doctor developed a close friendship that would last throughout her life. He also became her most trusted medical adviser. Over the years she wrote him letters from time to time, updating him on her various ailments and asking his advice for treatment.

Off her feet for a while

> *"She is a little doll alongside Diego. . . . People stop in their tracks to look in wonder."*

Although her name is listed as "Frida" on her birth certificate, Kahlo grew up using the German spelling of her name, "Frieda." But in the late 1930s, with the rise of Nazism in Germany, she dropped the e. The Nazi Party, under dictator Adolf Hitler, took control of Germany in 1933. Hitler's goal was to take over the world. Nazis believed in the superiority of white, blue-eyed Germans and Europeans. They hated Jews, Gypsies, and other minorities and were against democracy, Communism, Socialism—any movement that promoted equality.

because of the pain, Kahlo began to paint again. In 1931 she completed *Frida and Diego Rivera*, a portrait of the two painted in a primitive style. Rivera overshadows his wife in the painting. Wearing heavy shoes, his feet are firmly planted on the floor. He holds a palette and paintbrushes tightly in his right hand, and he looks away from Kahlo. Both messages show her awareness that art was the top priority in her husband's life. Kahlo's feet are tiny in contrast to Rivera's and seem to barely touch the ground. Her head is tilted toward her husband, implying that she is his adoring wife. Her hand just barely clasps his, a sign that she knows she cannot control or possess him.

Another painting Kahlo completed in 1931 marked a turning point in the development of her unique style.

Frida and Diego Rivera. 1931. Oil on canvas. 39″ x 31½″.

It is a portrait of horticulturist Luther Burbank, who had died several years earlier. Burbank had spent his career of fifty-three years creating plant hybrids—that is, new kinds of fruits, vegetables, and trees. The plants he developed were hardier and more productive than the parent varieties. Kahlo was fascinated by Burbank's work. To her, he represented California's amazing variety of produce.[12] Her portrait is a tribute to Burbank's imagination and efforts to create better plants.

The portrait of Burbank is a departure from Kahlo's primitive style. It is not a realistic likeness. Instead, it is a fantasy work, showing Burbank himself as a hybrid—half man and half tree. The tree's roots are being fed by Burbank's skeleton, which is buried in the ground. The painting also introduces themes about the close connection between life and death that are frequently seen in Mexican folk art. They would become common themes in Kahlo's paintings as well.[13]

Rivera finished his work in San Francisco, and the couple returned to Mexico in June 1931. Kahlo was eager to go home, back to the "country of enchiladas and refried beans."[14] Despite her enjoyment of San Francisco, she resented the United States, with all its wealth and influence over her country. She wrote, "Every day, the ugly part of the United States steals a piece [of Mexico]."[15] Rivera was not as enthusiastic about their return to Mexico, but he had promised to complete a mural at the National Palace.[16]

With the money he made from his work in California,

Luther Burbank

Kahlo portrayed horticulturist Luther Burbank as half man, half tree. *Luther Burbank.* 1931. Oil on masonite, 34½″ x 24½″.

Rivera decided to build a new house for himself and his wife in the San Angel section of Mexico City. The flat-roofed, three-story contemporary structure was actually two houses. The larger one (for him) was painted pink. The other, for Kahlo, was painted blue. The two houses were connected by a bridge and surrounded by a fence of giant green cacti.

After Rivera and Kahlo settled in, she went back to her role as devoted wife. She learned how to cook her husband's favorite dishes with the help of his former wife, Lupe Marín. By this time, the two women had become good friends. Kahlo also resumed taking lunch to her husband at work at the National Palace every day. But the couple was not destined to stay in Mexico for very long. Rivera's presence would soon be requested in the United States once again.

Rivera had a little bridge built to connect his and Kahlo's homes.

6

Diary on Canvas

In the years since the Mexican Revolution, interest in Mexico and what was termed the country's renaissance, or rebirth, had grown. People in the United States applauded the gains the Mexican government was making to help the country and its people.

Reflecting that interest in Mexico, a group of prominent New York businesspeople and patrons of the arts had met at the New York home of John D. Rockefeller Jr. on December 9, 1930. Their purpose was to create an organization, to be known as the Mexican Art Association, Inc., to cultivate artistic and cultural fellowship between the United States and Mexico.[1]

To promote that goal, the committee decided to give Diego Rivera—who was by this time among the most famous artists in the world—a one-man show at the newly established Museum of Modern Art in New York City. The museum, founded in 1929, is considered one of the finest museums in the world for contemporary paintings, sculpture, and other artwork.

Rivera was ecstatic. He considered an exhibition at the Museum of Modern Art to be "the pinnacle of professional success [for an artist]."[2] Indeed, his would be only the second one-man show the museum had hosted to that point. The first was an exhibition of the works of French painter Henri Matisse.

Rivera and Kahlo arrived in New York by boat in November 1931. As in San Francisco, Rivera was treated like a celebrity. The couple was entertained in high style at parties and receptions during their five-month stay. They also met many of New York's top businesspeople and art collectors.

Rivera's show opened on December 23, 1931. It included a wide variety of his work—almost 150 works in oils and watercolors, along with a number of drawings and sketches. The focal point of the exhibit was a collection of seven movable frescoes created specially for the exhibit.

Rivera's exhibit was well received by critics, although there was some controversy over several pieces that seemed to criticize New York.[3] The most offensive, *Frozen Assets*, portrays New York life in layers. At the top of the painting, skyscrapers tower over masses of working people crammed in subways. In the middle of the painting, homeless people huddle on a wharf while a tough-looking policeman keeps a menacing watch over them. The lowest layer shows a woman depositing her

Fresco Painting

Fresco is the Italian word for "fresh." Fresco painting involves applying watercolors to wet, or freshly made, plaster. As the plaster dries, it undergoes a chemical reaction with the air, which makes the colors especially vibrant. It is an ancient technique, dating back thousands of years. Some of the world's most famous frescoes are those that were uncovered in Pompeii, Italy. The city had been buried by volcanic ash from Mount Vesuvius in A.D. 79, and remained so for about seventeen centuries. The ash preserved the city, including much of its artwork.

jewels in a bank vault, which serves as the foundation for the city.

The criticism Rivera's work received only added to the public's interest in the exhibition. In its month at the museum, almost fifty-seven thousand people paid to see it, breaking all attendance records up to that time.

As with San Francisco, Kahlo had mixed feelings about New York and the people she met there. On the one hand, the couple was honored by the upper crust of New York's society and treated to the city's best entertainment. Yet Kahlo missed the simplicity and familiarity of her life at home. And while the wealth of the city was impressive, it also made her angry. The United States was in its third year of the Great Depression, and Kahlo was furious about the wide gap she saw between New York's wealthy few and the masses of poor people struggling to survive.[4]

Unlike the socialites who entertained her, Kahlo did not like going to plays or classical music concerts. Her tastes were simple. She preferred going to movies. *The Three Stooges* and *Tarzan* were two of her favorites. She also liked to shop. She was especially taken with five-and-dime stores, which sold a wide variety of products at low prices.

By April 1932, Rivera had another assignment lined up. This time he would be working in Detroit, Michigan. He was asked to paint a mural in the glass-ceilinged courtyard of the Detroit Institute of Arts. The theme for the mural would be the glorification of industry. It would show the power, progress, and importance of machinery in the modern world. Funding the project was Edsel Ford, president of the Ford Motor Company and head of the Detroit Arts Committee. He was the son of Henry Ford, the businessman responsible for developing assembly lines for the mass production of automobiles.

Rivera had long been fascinated by machinery and its possibilities for changing and improving life.[5] Detroit was considered the capital of industry in the United States, and Ford wanted Rivera to cover the full scope of the city's industry. Along with automobiles, the murals were to include Detroit's pharmaceutical, chemical, and steel industries.

Kahlo traveled with Rivera to San Francisco and New York, but she did not like the United States, calling it "Gringolandia."

Rivera working on a panel of *Detroit Industry* at the Detroit Institute of Art.

To prepare, Rivera spent his first three months in the city doing research. He immersed himself in Detroit's industries, visiting factories, machine shops, and laboratories. He wanted to fill his mind with images of production, which he would then transform into murals. Rivera made thousands of sketches of blast furnaces, conveyor belts, chemical laboratories, and assembly rooms. "I was afire with enthusiasm," he wrote later.[6]

As for Kahlo, she was even less impressed with Detroit than she had been with New York. Lonely, she missed her family, along with the spicy food she so enjoyed.[7] She saw Detroit as dirty and dismal, with no color or style. The weather in the summer of 1932 added to her displeasure, because she was hotter and more uncomfortable than at home.

Kahlo was also pregnant. She had a difficult first few months, fighting nausea and weakness. She was worried about the baby she was carrying. Although she desperately wanted to have a child, she feared that with her injuries from the bus accident, having a baby might kill her.

Kahlo wrote to her friend Dr. Eloesser, asking his

advice about the pregnancy. Before she could receive his reply, she suffered a painful miscarriage in July. She was rushed to Henry Ford Hospital, where she stayed for the next thirteen days. Her heart was broken with the loss of the baby, and she descended into a deep depression.[8]

Two months after her miscarriage, Kahlo was dealt another blow. She received word that her mother, who had been diagnosed with breast cancer six months earlier, was near death. She rushed back to Coyoacán, where her mother died a week later. Kahlo stayed in Mexico for another month, visiting with her family and dealing with her grief.

Back in Detroit, Kahlo faced the winter of 1932 in a poor state of mind. The weather was cold and dreary, and she felt overcome with sadness over the loss of her baby and her mother. Rivera was not available to provide emotional support, as he was working up to fifteen hours a day, seven days a week, on his murals.

Once again, Kahlo turned to painting to vent her feelings. This time, she created what would be considered one of her most distinguished works, *Henry Ford Hospital*. It is small, just over twelve inches by fifteen inches, painted in oils on tin. It shows a woman, presumably Kahlo herself, suffering a miscarriage. In the distance, a Ford automobile plant seems to coldly dismiss her suffering. Six symbolic objects that represent her feelings float around her body, connected to her by veinlike red ribbons.

Despite its graphic brutality, the painting represented

an extremely original way to express her reality and her feelings. It showed a woman's ability to deal with life's cruelty and to endure physical and emotional pain. About the painting, Rivera wrote, "Never before had a woman put such agonized poetry on canvas as Frida did at this time in Detroit."[9]

The painting was done in a style that reflected Mexican folk art *retablos*, anonymous paintings that are about the size of a postcard. The purpose of a *retablo* was to show a miracle and to honor the deity or saint who was responsible for it. Kahlo had begun to collect *retablos*, which she found fascinating.[10]

> *"Never before had a woman put such agonized poetry on canvas as Frida did at this time in Detroit."*

These small paintings were usually created on tin, copper, or cloth. Usually very colorful, *retablos* were normally made up of three parts. At the top would be the divine figure who was responsible for the miracle. Within the Catholic tradition it usually was God, a saint, or the Virgin Mary. The middle portion of the *retablo* showed the event itself, in which a life-threatening disease or disastrous event was prevented or stopped. At the bottom would be an inscription giving the name, date, and place of the miracle. By painting on tin and using a variation of the *retablo* format, Kahlo was attempting to honor this Mexican folk art style.

Also in 1932, Kahlo painted *Self-Portrait on the Border Line Between Mexico and the United States*. The work, approximately eleven inches by thirteen inches, shows her dressed in an elegant pink dress and holding a Mexican flag in one hand. In her other hand she holds a cigarette, which appears in stark contrast to her fine attire. She stands on a stone boundary, which represents the border between the United States and Mexico. The painting portrays Mexico's rich heritage and natural beauty. In contrast, the United States is shown as a land of cold machinery, skyscrapers, and smokestacks.

Kahlo was expressing her disgust for the United States and its culture. She viewed the United States, with the sterility of its machinery and industry, in direct contrast to the natural beauty of Mexico, where traditional values were respected and people made their living from the land rather than in factories.

Kahlo completed *My Birth* in 1932 as well. Painted on tin, it is a graphic representation of her mother giving birth to her in their home in Coyoacán. As on a *retablo*, the bottom of the painting includes space for an inscription. Yet it remains blank, indicating that she had nothing to say; that this birth was no miracle.

Rivera's murals in Detroit were unveiled in March 1933. They were huge depictions honoring science, industry, and labor. Yet they immediately created controversy. Some people in Detroit viewed them as sacrilegious, while others believed that they promoted Communism. Still others said they were indecent.

Rivera's critics wanted the murals removed. Yet Rivera's patron, Edsel Ford, weathered the storm and supported the artist. "I admire Rivera's spirit," he said. "I really believe he was trying to express his idea of the spirit of Detroit."[11] The murals remained, and are still there today.

By this time, Kahlo had spent so much time in the United States that she was getting comfortable enough to express her full personality. While in Detroit, she occasionally behaved outrageously. She especially enjoyed shocking the society matrons who entertained her from time to time. She viewed them as boring, snobby, and stupid.[12] In direct defiance to their conservative, midwestern culture and values, Kahlo took delight in speaking her mind. She promoted Communism and criticized the Catholic Church. She also used coarse language at times, all the while pretending that she did not know the meaning of her offensive words. Her behavior amused her husband, who enjoyed seeing his spirited wife express herself.[13]

7

Going Home

With his work in Detroit completed, Rivera's next job was back in New York City. He had been asked by Nelson Rockefeller, son of business tycoon John D. Rockefeller Jr., to paint a mural in the lobby of the newly constructed RCA (Radio Corporation of America) building at Rockefeller Center.

Rivera and Kahlo returned to New York in late March 1933. Kahlo was pleased to be able to renew the friendships made during her earlier time there, and she felt comfortable returning to familiar territory.

The title of the RCA mural was *Man at the Crossroads Looking with Hope and High Vision to the Choosing of a New and Better Future*. Rivera's intention was to show the links between industry, science, capitalism, and Communism. The mural would be prominently displayed above the elevators facing the building's entrance.

Rivera immediately went to work; he only had two

> ## Nelson Rockefeller
>
> In the 1860s, the Rockefeller family began building its fortune in the oil and steel industries. The Rockefellers soon became known for philanthropy, establishing several colleges and museums, including Colonial Williamsburg in Virginia. Nelson Rockefeller continued his family's legacy. He revamped the State University of New York (SUNY), created many of New York's highways, and, with his friend Roy Neuberger, built a museum on the campus of SUNY Purchase College. He also entered into public service. After holding several positions in the federal government, he became governor of New York (1958–1973). From 1974 to 1976, he served as vice president of the United States under Gerald Ford. His treatment of Rivera over the mural in Rockefeller Center is still a subject of controversy.

months to complete the project before the building would open. Another ambitious undertaking, this mural would be sixty-three feet long. When Rivera began to paint, people visited the site and paid to watch him as he worked.[1]

When he was almost finished with the mural, controversy began to develop over its content. Many people were upset because the mural seemed to praise Communism over capitalism. With New York City as one of the world's leading centers for capitalism and trade, that seemed insulting. In the mural, Rivera had painted Soviet Russia's first government head, Vladimir Lenin, as the leader of the workers. In addition, he used the color red, which represented Communism, predominantly throughout the mural. The work also conveyed the extravagance of the rich in America. In contrast, masses of jobless workers were shown being attacked by police. For many, the result was a criticism of American industry and way of life, and a tribute to Communism.

On April 24, 1934, a headline in the *New York World-Telegram* newspaper read, "RIVERA PAINTS SCENES OF COMMUNIST ACTIVITY AND JOHN D. [ROCKEFELLER] JR. FOOTS THE BILL."[2] The reporter had seen the mural and interviewed Rivera. Nelson Rockefeller, who had commissioned the work, also was not pleased with the mural's content. At a minimum, he insisted that Rivera must paint over Lenin's face and replace it with the face of an unknown man.

Rivera refused. In his autobiography, he wrote that Rockefeller's request was "reasonable." Even so, he would not comply, stating that "one change might lead to demands for others."[3] A two-week standoff began between the two men, with neither willing to budge.

On May 9, guards marched into the RCA building. They formed a line in front of the scaffolding where Rivera was working. He was called down, given payment for his work, and told that his services were no longer needed. Carpenters began building a screen to hide the mural from view. Armed guards blocked Rivera from returning to the building.

Rivera's supporters were furious that his artistic freedom of expression was being denied. They set up picket lines in front of Rockefeller Center and at Rockefeller's home, demanding that the artist be allowed to finish his work as he saw fit. Mounted police were summoned to keep order. Rockefeller assured Rivera he would not harm the work. A year later, in the dead of night, the mural would be destroyed, reviving people's outrage.

Kahlo and Rivera at Jones Beach, Long Island, New York, in 1933.

Toward the end of their stay in New York, Kahlo began to paint again too. Her new work, which she would complete back in Mexico, was called *My Dress Hangs There*. It is a dense collage of symbols, all used to express her disdain for American lifestyles and values. She shows a golf trophy and a toilet, each atop a classic Greek column. She uses them as symbols to show America's dependence on convenience and obsession with athletic competitions, which she thought were trivial. A telephone sits on top of a skyscraper, showing the importance of instant communication in American life. A garbage bin overflows with trash, implying the wastefulness of American society. In another spot, a church is shown with a dollar sign intertwined around a cross. Still another section shows a gasoline pump, which she uses to criticize America's dependence on automobiles. In the center of the chaotic display hangs one of Kahlo's colorful Tehuana dresses. It stands as a symbol of the purity and simplicity of Mexican life and values in contrast with the decadence and superficiality of life in America. Kahlo's absence from her dress shows that while she may physically be in America, her heart and spirit are Mexican.[4]

After nine months in New York City, Kahlo was homesick and ready to return to her home. But Rivera did not want to leave; he loved the United States and wanted to continue to paint there. The couple had violent arguments over the issue, until Rivera finally relented. The couple headed back to Mexico City in late 1933.

Frida Kahlo

My Dress Hangs There. 1933. Oil and collage on masonite, 18″ x 19¾″.

They settled again into their San Angel home. Kahlo was happy to be there, but Rivera was depressed. Missing the attention and celebrity he had received in the United States, he moped around and refused to work. He blamed his wife for spoiling his time in the limelight. Without his income, the couple's finances became increasingly tight, causing further household stress.

In 1934, Rivera revived a bit and began painting nudes. One of his models was Kahlo's younger sister, Cristina. She and Frida were less than a year apart in age and had always enjoyed a close relationship.

Later that year, however, Kahlo discovered to her horror that her husband was having an affair with Cristina. Kahlo had been aware of his relationships with many of his models and assistants during the course of their marriage. While his affairs caused her deep distress, she continued to love her husband and to stay with him. But this was different. She saw this as the ultimate insult for him to betray her with her own sister.

In a letter to a friend, Kahlo wrote, "I had never suffered so much and did not think I could take so much pain. You know better than anyone what Diego means to me in all senses, and on the other hand, she was the sister whom I loved the most and whom I tried to help as much

> **"I had never suffered so much and did not think I could take so much pain."**

as I could."[5] Kahlo left their San Angel home in early 1935 and moved into an apartment in Mexico City. In an effort to express her disgust and anguish, she stopped wearing her Tehuana outfits and cut off the long black hair that Rivera loved. She hardly knew how to deal with her rage over her husband's and sister's betrayal.

As one response to her pain, Kahlo painted one of her best-known works in 1935, called *A Few Small Nips*. Kahlo got the idea for the painting from a newspaper story about a man who brutally stabbed his girlfriend. In court, the man defended himself by saying, "But I only gave her a few small nips!"[6]

Later that year Kahlo traveled to New York City to escape her misery in Mexico and to get comfort and support from her friends there. Eventually, with the space of time and distance, she was able to forgive her husband and her sister.

8

Torn Apart

Kahlo returned to Mexico from New York in the late summer of 1935. After her husband's affair with her sister Cristina, Kahlo began to have brief affairs of her own. Rivera was not concerned about his wife's affairs with women. But he became extremely jealous if he found out that she was having an affair with a man. To avoid a possibly violent confrontation between her husband and a lover, Kahlo did her best to keep her relationships with other men secret.[1]

In 1936, Kahlo painted her family tree, calling it *My Grandparents, My Parents, and I*. In the painting, she appears in the foreground as a healthy two-year-old child. She is standing in the courtyard of her home in Coyoacán, looking directly and confidently at her viewer. In her hand, the young Kahlo holds a long red ribbon, which represents her bloodline. It connects her to her parents and grandparents. Guillermo's and Matilde's portraits appear behind her. She copied their likenesses from their wedding photograph. Kahlo positions herself directly in front of her father to show their close relationship when she was a child. Her mother's parents float above a Mexican landscape, complete with cacti, brush, and rocky volcanic mountains, indicating her Mexican heritage. The portraits of her father's parents hover above the ocean that separated them, in Europe, from Mexico.

In January 1937, Leon Trotsky and his wife, Natalia, arrived in Mexico as guests of Rivera and Kahlo. Trotsky, along with Vladimir Lenin, had been at the forefront of the Russian Revolution in 1917. Trotsky had served as Lenin's closest adviser. At Lenin's death in 1924, however, Josef Stalin rose to power and took Lenin's place. Jealous of Trotsky's influence in the country, Stalin forced him out of the Communist Party in 1927. The next year, Stalin exiled Trotsky to Soviet Central Asia and in 1929 deported him to Turkey. Trotsky and his wife also found refuge in Norway. A decade later, Lenin called for Trotsky's assassination.

Rivera knew that Trotsky needed another country in which to live. He appealed to the Mexican government on Trotsky's behalf, and officials agreed to let the Trotskys live in Mexico. Leon Trotsky and his wife moved into Kahlo's house in Coyoacán, where they would stay for the next two years. To ensure their safety from potential assassins, Rivera added barricades around the house. He also hired armed guards to protect the couple.

Self-Portrait Dedicated to Leon Trotsky. 1937. Oil on masonite, 30″ x 24″.

Leon Trotsky, age fifty-seven, was a tall, dashing figure with a magnetic personality. Kahlo served as the Trotskys' primary host and guide during their stay in Mexico. After about six months Kahlo, age thirty, and Trotsky began having an affair, which lasted only a couple of months. Afterward, the two remained friends. For his birthday in November, Kahlo presented Trotsky with a portrait of herself.

The years 1937 and 1938 were artistically productive for Kahlo. She finished more work during that time than in the previous eight years combined. Among the works she created were *Me and My Doll* (1937), which suggests her frustration at not being able to have children.[2] She also painted her only portrait of her husband, though he does appear as part of her other paintings.

Another 1937 piece was *Fulang-Chang and I*, which shows her with one of her favorite pet spider monkeys. Kahlo loved animals and had a number of exotic pets over the years. Along with spider monkeys she kept parrots, eagles, deer, peacocks, and dogs.

In 1938 she painted another important work, *What the Water Gave Me*. This fantasy painting shows Kahlo's feet in a bathtub as if she were looking at them while taking a bath. The tub is filled with a number of symbols representing different events in her life. Also that year, Kahlo participated in a group art exhibition at the University Gallery in Mexico City. It was the first time her work was displayed publicly.

Fulang-Chang and I, 1937, was placed in a painted folk-art mirror frame a couple of years later. Oil on masonite, 15¾″ x 11″ (without frame).

In 1938, American actor and art collector Edward G. Robinson paid a visit to Rivera and Kahlo while he was vacationing in Mexico. Along with his own work, Rivera took the opportunity to show Robinson some of his wife's paintings. Robinson was impressed and bought four of her pieces for $200 each. Before that, Kahlo had just given her paintings away. With this first sale, she began to consider the possibility that her work might be important and valuable in the art world.[3]

In April 1938, Rivera and Kahlo hosted another visitor to their country, André Breton. A French writer and poet, Breton was responsible for starting the Surrealist movement in literature and art in 1924. Breton had come to Mexico to meet with Leon Trotsky and to immerse himself in Mexican culture. He and his wife would spend several months there, staying most of the time at Rivera's home in San Angel.

Surrealism

Surrealism began as a new way of writing poetry. Its purpose was to focus on the realm of dreams and the subconscious mind, rather than on reality. The poets would write whatever came to mind, and they would not change their words later. They viewed their words as pure creation. The movement spilled over into art, where strange combinations of objects, people, and events were presented as if seen in a dream.

Kahlo did not like Breton; she thought he was "pretentious and boring."[4] Breton, on the other hand, found both Kahlo and her paintings fascinating. He later wrote, "My surprise and joy was unbounded when I discovered, on my arrival in Mexico, that her work has blossomed forth,

> **"They thought I was a Surrealist, but I wasn't. I never painted dreams. I painted my own reality."[5]**

in her latest paintings, into pure surreality, despite the fact that it had been conceived without any prior knowledge whatsoever of the ideas motivating the activities of my friends and myself."[6] Suggesting the power and drama of her work, Breton later wrote, "The art of Frida Kahlo is a ribbon around a bomb."[7] Before he left Mexico, Breton offered to organize a one-woman exhibition of Kahlo's work in Paris the next year.

In the meantime, a collector of modern art in New York City, Julien Levy, contacted Kahlo about presenting an exhibition of her work at his gallery there. Someone familiar with her paintings had told him about them, and he wrote Kahlo to ask if she would send photographs of some of her work so that he could assess it.

Kahlo was not sure she wanted to do the show. She feared rejection and embarrassment if her work was not well received.[8] Up to this time she had painted only for herself or to create a gift for a friend, rather than for the public. Because her work was so personal, she could not see why other people would be interested in it.[9]

Still, she mailed Levy some photographs of her paintings, and he moved forward with plans for what would be Kahlo's first one-woman exhibition. Held in November 1938, it included twenty-five of her pieces.

Despite her fears, the Kahlo exhibit was well received by art critics and art collectors. It also got good coverage in the newspapers. By the time the show was over, she had sold half of her exhibition pieces and had requests for more paintings.

While in New York, Kahlo had one of her few serious relationships outside her marriage to Rivera. She fell in love with Nickolas Muray, a Hungarian-born photographer whom she had met earlier in Mexico. Handsome, charming, and sophisticated, Muray helped plan Kahlo's exhibition, and he stole her heart. Even so, her underlying devotion to Rivera remained intact.[10]

> *Her work was so personal, she could not see why the public would have any interest in it.*

From New York, Kahlo went to Paris, France, to prepare for her show there. She arrived in January 1939 expecting that André Breton had the event organized. Instead, to her dismay, she found that her paintings had not yet been admitted into the country, and no gallery was booked for her show.[11] Over the next two months, the plans finally began to fall into place. The exhibit was held at the Pierre Colle Gallery. Rather than being a one-woman show as she had expected, however, it turned into a display of a variety of Mexican art. The exhibit included pre-Columbian artifacts and Mexican folk art, along with seventeen of Kahlo's paintings. Titled Mexique, the show opened in March 1939.

Although her work did not sell well in Paris, Kahlo received high praise from art critics and important artists of the day, including Vasily Kandinsky, Marcel Duchamp, and Pablo Picasso. In addition, the Louvre, one of the best-known and respected art galleries in the world, bought one of her paintings, *The Frame*, to add to its collection. It was the museum's first acquisition of a work by a twentieth-century Mexican artist. Rivera was proud of his wife's critical success in Paris. He later wrote, "In mere weeks, Frida won over the Parisian world of art more completely than more famous painters had after years of struggle."[12]

By this time, Kahlo was beginning to feel some of the same sense of celebrity that her husband had enjoyed for years. While in Paris, Italian fashion designer Elsa Schiaparelli created a line of dresses called *La Robe Madame Rivera*, which were inspired by Kahlo's Tehuana costumes. In addition, Kahlo's hands, covered as usual with Mexican rings, were photographed for the cover of *Vogue* fashion magazine.

Although she thought the city of Paris was beautiful, Kahlo did not enjoy the people. In one of her letters to

Muray, she criticized Parisians as pompous, pretentious, and self-absorbed. She wrote, "[Parisians] are so . . . 'intellectual' and rotten that I can't stand them anymore. They sit for hours in the 'cafes' . . . and talk without stopping . . . thinking themselves the gods of the world."[13]

Upon leaving Paris, Kahlo returned briefly to New York, where she was hoping to continue her relationship with Muray. However, by that time he had fallen in love with another woman, whom he would eventually marry. Crushed by his change of feelings toward her, Kahlo left New York to go back to Mexico.

Kahlo's anguish was only deepened upon her return to Rivera. The ten years of his infidelity had taken their toll on her; their relationship was in shambles. Kahlo left their San Angel home in July 1939 and moved back into her family home in Coyoacán, where she would live for the remainder of her life. By the fall, Rivera had filed for divorce.

The reason Rivera gave for wanting a divorce was that he could no longer continue to hurt his wife with his many romantic relationships outside their marriage. "I began taking stock of myself as a marriage partner," he later wrote. "I found very little which could be said in my favor. I loved her too much to want to cause her suffering."[14] Others have suggested that Rivera may have found out about Kahlo's affairs with Trotsky or Muray, which caused him to want to leave her.[15] At any rate, the divorce became final in December.

Kahlo showed her anguish over the breakup with Rivera in *Self-Portrait with Cropped Hair*. Dressed in a man's suit, she holds the scissors that cut off all her long hair. 1940. Oil on canvas, 15¾″ x 11″.

Kahlo works on *The Two Fridas*, a double portrait of the Frida loved by Rivera sitting alongside the Frida he did not love. Rivera's beloved Frida, on the right, wears traditional Mexican clothes. The other Frida is in a European dress.

Kahlo, devastated by the separation and divorce from her beloved Rivera, sank into deep depression and began drinking heavily. She deteriorated physically as well, fighting a fungal infection in her right hand, along with renewed back pain. She came under the care of Dr. Juan Farill, who prescribed rest, along with a contraption that included a forty-pound weight, which was used to stretch her spine several hours each day.

Deep in mental and physical pain, Kahlo began to

paint again. By the time her divorce was final, she had completed what would become one of her best-known works, *The Two Fridas*. It was her first large painting, measuring sixty-seven square inches. Reflecting her unhappiness at her separation from Rivera, the painting consists of a double self-portrait, with two images of herself sitting side by side. One is dressed in a Tehuana outfit and holds a miniature portrait of Rivera as a boy. That Frida represents the independent, free-spirited part of her that Rivera loved. The other Frida wears a lacy white Victorian dress. This side stands for the traditional part of herself that expected Rivera's fidelity—the part of her that Rivera no longer loved. Both Fridas' hearts are exposed, expressing her deep pain and vulnerability. A vein flows from the portrait of Rivera and encircles both Fridas. With surgical pincers, the Victorian Frida attempts to stop the flow of blood that threatens to drain her of life. As in all her self-portraits, the faces are stoic and unemotional, but the background of this painting shows a stormy sky, which suggests the underlying anger that is being suppressed.[16]

9

Coming to Terms

"Let me tell you kid, that this time has been the worst in my whole life and I am surprised that one can live through it," wrote Kahlo in a letter describing her mental state after her divorce.[1] Kahlo created some of her best work during that period of her life, as she expressed her feelings on canvas. At the same time, without Rivera's financial support, she needed the money her paintings would bring in. She had both her living expenses and her continual medical expenses. Friends came to her aid, either lending her money or buying her paintings to help her get by.[2]

Despite their divorce, Kahlo and Rivera maintained frequent contact with each other. She handled his business transactions and correspondence, and the couple continued to entertain and attend public events together.

In June 1940, Rivera left Mexico for San Francisco. He had been commissioned to paint a mural there for the San Francisco Junior College as part of the Golden Gate International Exposition. Meanwhile, Kahlo's health continued to decline. By September 1940, she was so ill that Rivera urged her to come to San Francisco. He wanted Dr. Eloesser to evaluate her condition and advise her about having more surgery.[3]

In San Francisco, Kahlo was confined in a hospital for a month under Dr. Eloesser's care. In addition to giving Kahlo medical care, Eloesser also spoke with both Rivera and Kahlo separately about the possibility of their reconciliation.

He told Rivera that Kahlo's health declined when they were apart.[4] Once Kahlo was feeling better, Eloesser approached her as well, suggesting that she might consider the possibility of reuniting with her husband. Eloesser shared his opinion that some men were incapable of fidelity in marriage and that Rivera would never change. To take him back, Eloesser said, she would have to accept that reality.

Eloesser's efforts paid off. Rivera and Kahlo agreed to get back together and were remarried on December 8, 1940, the date of Rivera's fifty-fourth birthday. From that point forward, their relationship grew calmer, for the most part. Rivera became almost like a child to Kahlo, and she continued to love him despite his faults. In turn, Rivera loved being babied. He had never cared much about personal hygiene, and Kahlo was even known to give her husband baths, coaxing him with a tub filled with bath toys to play with.

Despite the difficulties of their relationship, Kahlo and Rivera loved each other deeply and decided to try marriage for a second time.

The couple began a generally peaceful phase in their relationship that met each of their needs and would last for the next fourteen years.[5] Both continued to have extramarital affairs. Kahlo taught herself to accept her husband's infidelities, and she kept hers secret from him. In 1941, she wrote in a letter to Dr. Eloesser, "Remarriage is working well. Small amounts of arguing, greater mutual understanding, and, on my part, fewer obnoxious-type investigations regarding other ladies who suddenly occupy a preponderant place in his heart. I finally learned that life is so and the rest is unimportant."[6]

Kahlo lived in the Blue House in Coyoacán. Rivera stayed at his San Angel home, but he was often at the Blue House and maintained a bedroom there as well. Living in her family home gave Kahlo a sense of independence and peace, and she set about making it her place of sanctuary. She had the wooden floors painted a cheerful shade of yellow. She also surrounded herself with her favorite things—her collection of *retablos*, along with her many dolls and toys. In addition, giant papier-mâché Judas figures were placed throughout the house. A part of Mexican culture, they represented death. Despite their bright colors, to many they were ugly and frightening to look at.[7] Kahlo cherished them. Sometimes she even dressed them in her clothes in an effort to laugh at her own mortality.

> *Living in her family home gave Kahlo a sense of independence and peace.*

Kahlo typically spent her days painting, shopping, cooking, and taking care of her home, all activities that she enjoyed. Her many pets, which roamed freely through the house and courtyard, made her feel needed and helped take the place of the children she would never have.[8] Kahlo also corresponded with her friends, especially those in New York, writing charming letters full of news, gossip, humor, and affection.

At the same time, she loved to entertain friends and cook special dishes, buying fresh ingredients at the Coyoacán market within walking distance of her home. A frequent guest was her sister Cristina and her children, Isolda and Antonio. A visit with their Aunt Frida was special, because she gave them lots of attention and told them funny stories.

Kahlo's father died of a heart attack in 1941, which brought sadness into her contented life.[9] The next year she began a diary, recording her reflections and memories of her childhood and teenage years, along with her day-to-day thoughts and impressions. Kahlo illustrated the diary with many imaginative drawings and sketches that further conveyed her feelings.

From 1942 to 1944, one of Rivera's teenage daughters, Guadalupe, from his marriage to Lupe Marín, lived with Kahlo in the Blue House. She later wrote about her life there with Kahlo: "Living with Frida was an education in itself. I learned about cultural values I had been ignorant about until then. She accepted me without reservation into the heart of her daily life."[10]

Over the years, guests flocked to the Blue House. People were drawn to Kahlo because of her sense of fun, her sincerity, and her genuineness. She delighted in parties and was quick with a hearty laugh. "Only Frida's laughter was loud enough to rise above [the music of the mariachis]," wrote Guadalupe.[11]

Kahlo and her *Self-Portrait as a Tehuana*. 1943. Oil on masonite, 24¾″ x 24″. She painted a tiny portrait of Rivera on her forehead.

Kahlo not only entertained family and friends; she and her husband were also regularly visited by celebrities, art collectors, and intellectuals from the United States, Mexico, and Europe. Guests usually gathered in Kahlo's kitchen, where the stove was set in blue, white, and yellow tiles, with clay pots and copper kettles hanging above. For dinner, Kahlo would cut fresh flowers from her courtyard to grace the table as a centerpiece. During dinner, Rivera liked to make controversial statements to annoy his guests. In response, Kahlo would lighten the tension with funny stories and jokes. Along with lots of food, the evenings usually included plenty of tequila, and ended with everyone united in singing Mexican folk ballads and patriotic songs.

National and religious holidays were special times for Kahlo. One of her favorites was Posadas at Christmas. Posadas is a festival that recreates the story of Mary and Joseph's search for a place where Mary could give birth to Jesus. Groups go from house to house singing and asking for a room at an inn (*posada*) for the night.

"During the time I lived with her and my father," Guadalupe wrote, "[Frida] followed the traditional practices down to the last detail. From Diego's birthday [December 8] to February 2, the doors of the Blue House stood wide open to children, neighbors, the rowdy Kahlo family, and any friends who lived in the area."[12]

With Kahlo living in the Blue House, Rivera had a

Pre-Columbian Art

Pre-Columbian refers to the time in the Americas before 1492, when explorer Christopher Columbus arrived, bringing European influences. Pre-Columbian art was made by any of the indigenous peoples of Mexico, Central, or South America. Some of these peoples were the Maya, the Aztec, and the Inca, but there were many other groups as well. Materials they used for their sculptures included gold, ceramic, wood, and stone.

large study added to the house, and it became her favorite room there.[13] He also installed a small, stepped pyramid in the courtyard to use as a showcase for displaying some of his pre-Columbian treasures.

In the 1940s, Kahlo's recognition as an artist began to grow.[14] Her previous exhibitions led to increasing exposure for her work in art circles. In 1942 her paintings were shown at New York's Museum of Modern Art in an exhibition called "Twentieth-Century Portraits." The next year she participated in an exhibit of works by thirty-one female artists at the Art of This Century Gallery in New York City. Also in 1943, her paintings appeared in an exhibition of Mexican Art at the Philadelphia Museum of Art, as well as in a group show at the Benjamin Franklin Library in Mexico City.

In 1943, Kahlo accepted a part-time teaching position at the School of Painting and Sculpture in Mexico City.

The school was for high school students with artistic talent who could not afford to attend art school. While the institute charged no fees, its faculty of twenty-two were among Mexico's best-known artists. Located on Esmeralda Street, the school was affectionately nick-named "La Esmeralda."

As a teacher, Kahlo became popular with her students. She was easygoing and used unconventional teaching methods. One of her students later talked about Kahlo's first day at the school: "She appeared there all of a sudden like a stupendous flowering branch because of her joyfulness, kindness, and enchantment. The young people who were going to be her students . . . received her with true enthusiasm and emotion. 'Well, kids, let's go to work,' Kahlo said. 'I will be your so-called teacher, I am not any such thing, I only want to be your friend.'"[15] With that, she began teaching twelve classes each week.

Kahlo thrived on the interaction with her students.[16] In turn, they valued her for her noncritical teaching style. She offered her students advice, but only as her opinion. At the same time, she gave them lots of praise and encouragement.[17] Instead of teaching art rules and theory, she helped students learn to evaluate their own work. Rather than requiring them to copy the works of famous artists, she took her students on field trips to the streets of Mexico City and to nearby towns, telling them to sketch what they found interesting. *"Muchachos,"* one student remembered her saying, "locked up here in school we can't do anything. Let's go into the street.

Let's go and paint the life in the street."[18] Another student said, "She did not influence us through her way of painting, but through her way of living, of looking at the world and at people and at art. She made us feel and understand a certain kind of beauty in Mexico that we would not have realized by ourselves."[19]

After several months of teaching, Kahlo found that the trip from Coyoacán to Mexico City became too difficult to manage with her poor health. Instead, she invited her students to come to her home for instruction. She loved teaching them there and often served refreshments. Sometimes they would all go to a movie after class was over. As a project, she arranged for her students to paint a mural of town and country scenes on the wall of a bar, called *La Rosita*, near her home.

At first, many students traveled to Coyoacán for class, but after a while Kahlo's art students dwindled to just four. They proudly called themselves "Los Fridos." The little band of students would continue to take instruction from Kahlo for several more years.

By the mid-1940s, Kahlo's physical condition had deteriorated further, with severe pain in her right foot and her spine. In addition, she lost her appetite, which weakened her further.[20] She tried a number of different orthopedic corsets in an effort to get support for her back and relief from her pain. Some were made of steel or leather; most were made of plaster, which she decorated with colorful drawings, symbols, and even feathers.

Kahlo visited many doctors during this time, desperate

Kahlo was often confined to her bed.

for relief from her constant pain. At one point she spent a period of three months almost continually in a vertical position with sandbags tied to her feet in an attempt to straighten her spine.

She continued to paint as a release for her emotions and a distraction from her pain. In 1944 she painted *The Broken Column*, showing her upper body encased by steel bands. Nails pierce her face and body; tears stream down her face. In addition, her body is split vertically to reveal a broken and crumbling Greek column, which represents her spine. Her face shows strength and defiance in contrast to her body's weakness.

Also in 1944, Kahlo produced what is considered her best portrait of someone other than herself, *Portrait of Doña Rosita Morillo*. Her subject was an elderly woman, the mother of one of Kahlo's most enthusiastic patrons. The highly detailed painting portrays the aging white-haired woman as she knits. Her kindly face shows an inner strength and suggests the wisdom of her years.

Kahlo and Rivera celebrated their fifteenth wedding anniversary in 1944. Even though they had been separated for most of the year, they chose to honor their marriage with a big party. As a gift to her husband, Kahlo presented Rivera with *Diego and Frida 1929–1944*. The painting is an unusual composite portrait with half of his face and half of hers merged together. But the halves do not quite match up, implying the discord in their marriage. Their common neck is encircled by bare tree branches, another sign of the discord they had endured in their relationship.

The next year Kahlo painted *Moses*. This work represented her impressions of a 1939 book entitled *Moses and Monotheism* by Sigmund Freud, Austrian physician and founder of psychoanalysis. Moses was a biblical Hebrew prophet and leader of the Israelites, or the Jewish people. In the painting he represents all heroes, or special leaders.[21] Kahlo's work shows Moses' birth, surrounded by a collage of gods, along with a wide range of political, social, and religious leaders throughout history. They include Jesus; Napoléon Bonaparte I, emperor of France in the early nineteenth century;

In 1948, the year this photo was taken, Kahlo rejoined the Communist Party.

Gandhi, Indian nationalist leader; and Karl Marx, political philosopher and revolutionist. In 1946 Kahlo received one of five National Prize awards in Mexico for this painting.

Also in 1946, Kahlo traveled to New York City, where she had an operation on her spine to fuse four vertebrae. She remained in the hospital there for two months. Once back in Mexico, she was again bedridden and spent the next eight months wearing a steel corset. Yet her pain only increased. To cope, she became dependent on alcohol and prescription drugs. Discouraged about her deteriorating condition, she wrote, "No matter how much I do to play the strong one, there are times when I would like to throw in the sponge."[22] During that recovery period, Kahlo painted *Tree of Hope*.

Throughout her life, Kahlo had believed in Communism as the only hope for improving living conditions for poor, uneducated people. In 1948 she rejoined the Communist Party. She also became increasingly interested in using her art to promote Communism. She wrote, "Above all I want to transform it [my painting] into something useful for the Communist revolutionary movement. . . . I have to fight with all my strength to contribute the few positive things my health allows me to the revolution."[23]

In 1949 Kahlo completed another work, *The Love Embrace of the Universe, the Earth (Mexico), Diego, Me, and Señor Xólotl*. In this painting she cradles a naked, adult-sized Rivera in her arms like an infant. She added a third eye in the middle of his forehead, representing his all-seeing, all-knowing wisdom. The painting shows her as a nurturing mother, not only to Rivera, but to the baby she was never able to have. Her favorite dog, Señor Xólotl, sleeps contentedly nearby. Surrounding the peaceful scene are layers representing the additional love and support of her native Mexico and the universe at large. Despite the sense of comfort and well-being in the painting, Kahlo's suffering as a mother figure to her husband is represented by a large gash across her neck and chest.

A Life Remembered

Kahlo's health continued to decline. In 1950 she had another bone graft, which led to a serious infection, causing her to remain in the hospital for an entire year. Rivera often spent the night at the hospital in the room next to his wife's. He set up a film projector in her room so she could watch her favorite movies. Many friends and family members came to visit, decorating her room and cheering her up with gifts and gossip. All the while, Kahlo continued to transform her corsets into pieces of art, using lipstick and iodine when paint was not available.

About that time, Kahlo wrote in her diary, "I've been sick for a year now. Doctor Farill saved me. He brought me back the joy of life. I don't feel any pain. Only this . . . tiredness, and naturally, quite often, despair. A despair which no words can describe. I'm still eager to live. I've started to paint again."[1]

By this time her work began to drift from portraiture

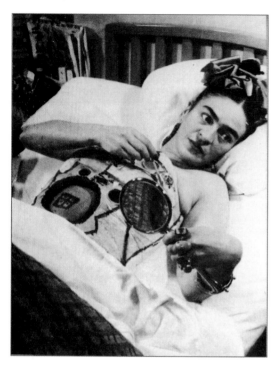

In the hospital in Mexico City, Kahlo painted decorations on the plaster corset that she had to wear.

to still lifes of fruits and vegetables, usually presented in provocative ways. Her style of painting began to change as well, probably due to the side effects from her heavy drug usage to numb her pain.[2] Rather than the very detailed work and fine, delicate lines of her earlier paintings, most of her last works were composed of rough, heavy strokes. They are generally not considered to be her best work.

In early 1953 Kahlo began to prepare for her first and only solo exhibition in Mexico, held on April 13 at the Gallery of Contemporary Art in Mexico City. Against her doctor's advice, she attended the event, arriving by ambulance and charming the guests from her canopied bed. By May, she was back in the hospital.

In July 1953, due to poor circulation, Kahlo's right foot developed gangrene, a condition in which the cells in the affected body part die. In August, to keep the gangrene from spreading throughout her body, doctors decided to amputate Kahlo's leg at the knee.

She dreaded the operation, but knew it was necessary. In her diary, she wrote, "I am very, very worried, but at the same time I feel it [the operation] would be a relief. In the hope that when I walk again I'll give what remains of my courage to Diego. Everything for Diego."[3] She also drew a sketch of her feet in her diary, with the caption, "Feet, what do I need them for if I have wings to fly."[4] After a three-month stay in the hospital, Kahlo was fitted with an artificial leg. It was uncomfortable, so she began to depend on crutches or a wheelchair.

The amputation was a turning point in Kahlo's life. After that she began to lose the will to continue her battles with her health. Rivera described her as "deeply depressed."[5] By February 1954, six months after the amputation, she wrote in her diary, "It seemed to me centuries of torture and at times I nearly went crazy. I still feel like committing suicide; Diego prevents me from doing it in the vain belief that maybe he will need me."[6]

In 1954 Kahlo completed the painting *Marxism Will Give Health to the Sick*. She appears in the work dressed in a plaster orthopedic corset, with a portrait of the revolutionist Karl Marx behind her. With one of his hands to support her, she throws away her crutch. At the same time, Marx's other hand crushes an American eagle, beneath which the mushroom cloud of

Toward the end of her life, Kahlo mostly painted small pictures like this one. *Still Life with Fruit*. 1942. Oil on sheet metal, 24¾" diameter.

an atomic bomb appears. The painting serves as a strong statement of her belief in the virtues of Communism over capitalism.

On July 2, 1954, Kahlo made her last public appearance. In her wheelchair, she went with Rivera to a political demonstration organized to denounce the United States and its interference in the politics of Guatemala. She carried a sign with a peace slogan, but she was not dressed in her usual Tehuana attire, and she looked tired.

A few days later, Kahlo celebrated her forty-seventh birthday with a big party at the Blue House. One hundred friends and family members came to honor her. Because of her weak condition, she had to be carried to the dining room to participate in the festivities.

Kahlo's last outing was a political demonstration. Rivera stood behind her, his hand on her shoulder.

After that, Kahlo was almost continuously bedridden and quickly declined. While she continued to dress in her Tehuana outfits each day, her usually upbeat personality took a serious downturn. She became irritable and short-tempered and suffered severe mood swings. She was easily annoyed, and her words could quickly become hateful. Sometimes she threw things at people from her bed if they made her angry.[7]

Despite her rapidly deteriorating condition, Kahlo and Rivera were still planning a big party to celebrate their upcoming twenty-fifth wedding anniversary. Kahlo's passion for her husband never waned. She told a friend, "For me he is my child, my son, my mother, my father, my husband, my everything."[8] She gave Rivera an antique gold ring as an anniversary gift. The next day, July 13, 1954, Kahlo died.

The official cause of Kahlo's death was a pulmonary embolism (the blockage of a blood vessel in the lungs), although many have suspected that she may have caused her death by taking an overdose of medication. Rivera was devastated by his loss, later writing, "July 13, 1954, was the most tragic day of my life. I had lost my beloved Frida forever."[9]

Kahlo's body, dressed in Tehuana costume and jewelry, lay in state in a gray coffin surrounded by red flowers at the Palace of Fine Arts in Mexico City. More than six hundred people filed past to pay their respects. The service turned into a political statement as well, when one of Kahlo's former students draped a Communist flag over her coffin.

From the viewing, the coffin was carried on the shoulders of her pallbearers, including Rivera, through the streets to the Panteón Civil de Dolores, a civil cemetery. There she was cremated, according to her wishes. As her body was placed on a cart to go into the crematory oven,

Capturing Kahlo on Film

In 2002, a major motion picture about Kahlo's life was released by Miramax. It was called *Frida* and starred Selma Hayek in the title role. A critical success, the movie introduced a broad audience to Frida Kahlo's life and work.

While this was the first major motion picture production about Kahlo, there have been a least ten documentaries made about her as well. Most of them are rather short, but some include archival footage of Kahlo. One of these is an hourlong documentary called *Frida Kahlo* (1982). Another, *Frida Kahlo and Tina Modotti* (1983), includes footage of Kahlo, Modotti, and Rivera.

those present sang her favorite Mexican songs. After the cremation, Kahlo's ashes were placed in a pre-Columbian urn and returned to the Blue House.

In 1958 Rivera had the Blue House and its contents turned into the Frida Kahlo Museum. His only request was "that a corner be set aside for me, alone, for whenever I felt the need to return to the atmosphere which recreated Frida's presence."[10] Today the museum continues to welcome visitors, who can view many of her paintings there, along with several by Rivera and others. The house remains very much as it was when Kahlo lived there. In her studio, an unfinished portrait of Josef Stalin appears on an easel, along with her diary and many personal items.

When she was well enough to be up, Kahlo painted here in her studio in the Blue House. On the easel is a portrait of Stalin that she had not completed.

It took thirty more years for Kahlo's work to become known and appreciated worldwide. With the rise of feminism in the late 1970s, Kahlo's paintings touched a deep chord with many women who could relate to her struggles with physical pain, along with her emotional

111

trials. Kahlo was also an inspiration to women because she had succeeded as an artist in the male-dominated art world.[11]

Today Kahlo is recognized as one of the great Mexican painters. In 1976, Kahlo's picture was chosen as the symbol for the International Year of the Woman. In 2001, her 1933 painting *Self-Portrait with Necklace* was chosen to appear on a United States stamp. The value of her paintings has skyrocketed as well, with *Self-Portrait with Monkey* selling at the prestigious Sotheby's auction house in London for $3.2 million in 1995.

Kahlo finished her last painting just eight days

Kahlo's personal photos and mementos are preserved and displayed at the Frida Kahlo Museum in Mexico City.

before her death. It was a still life of ripe watermelons, a symbol of life and vitality in Mexico. In the painting the fruit is off the vine, with several of the melons cut into pieces to display the luscious red fruit. Despite her physical decline and impending death, Kahlo painted the work in bright greens and reds, conveying a sense of hopefulness and cheer. In defiance of the physical and emotional pain she had endured thro-ughout her life, Kahlo's vibrant,

Kahlo is the first Hispanic woman to be honored on a U.S. stamp. It was unveiled here at the Phoenix Art museum in June 2001.

forthright spirit still dominated as she added the painting's title, *!Viva la Vida! (Long Live Life!)*

"I suffered two grave accidents in my life," Kahlo once said. "One in which a streetcar ran me over. . . . The other accident is Diego."[12] From the pain of both of those events, Kahlo's paintings emerged. She painted pictures of herself, for herself, as a way to express her emotions and forget her troubles. In doing so, Kahlo transformed her life into art, creating a collection of haunting images that continue to touch the world.

Chronology

1907—Magdalena Carmen Frida Kahlo y Calderón is born in Coyoacán, Mexico, on July 6.

1913—Contracts polio, which permanently affects her right leg.

1922—Begins high school at Mexico's National Preparatory School; meets muralist Diego Rivera.

1925—Suffers serious injuries in a bus accident.

1926—Completes her first painting, *Self-Portrait Wearing a Velvet Dress*.

1928—Meets Rivera again; asks him to assess her paintings; they begin a romantic relationship.

1929—Marries Rivera.

1930—Accompanies Rivera to San Francisco, California.

1931—Completes several portraits, including *Luther Burbank*; accompanies Rivera to New York City for his solo exhibition at the Museum of Modern Art.

1932—Goes with Rivera to Detroit, Michigan; suffers miscarriage; paints *Henry Ford Hospital;* mother dies of cancer; paints *My Birth*.

1933—Returns to New York while Rivera works on RCA Building mural; paints *My Dress Hangs There*.

1934—Discovers Rivera's affair with her sister Cristina.

1935—Separates from Rivera; paints *A Few Small Nips*.

1937—Allows Leon Trotsky and his wife to live in her home in Coyoacán during their exile from Russia; paints self-portrait for him.

1938—Participates in a group show in Mexico City, the first public exhibition of her work; paints *What the Water Gave Me;* travels to New York for the first solo exhibit of her work, held at the Julien Levy Gallery.

1939—Travels to Paris for participation in a group exhibition; she and Rivera divorce; paints *The Two Fridas*.

1940—Returns to San Francisco for medical treatment; remarries Rivera.

1941—Father dies.

1943—Begins teaching art at the School of Painting and Sculpture in Mexico City.

1944—Health begins to seriously decline; begins diary; paints *Diego and Frida 1929–1944* and *The Broken Column*.

1945—Paints *Moses*.

1946—Returns to New York for an operation on her spine; receives National Prize for *Moses*; paints *Tree of Hope* and *The Little Deer*.

1949—Paints *The Love Embrace of the Universe, the Earth (Mexico), Diego, Me, and Señor Xólotl*.

1950—Confined in a hospital for most of the year, recovering from a spinal infection.

1953—Has first solo exhibition in Mexico; right foot contracts gangrene and is amputated.

1954—Paints *Marxism Will Give Health to the Sick* and *!Viva la Vida!*; dies on July 13 from pulmonary embolism.

1958—Frida Kahlo Museum is established by Diego Rivera in the Blue House.

Chapter Notes

CHAPTER 1. TRIBUTE AT HOME

1. Martha Zamora, Marilyn Sode Smith, trans., *Frida Kahlo: The Brush of Anguish* (San Francisco: Chronicle Books, 1990), pp. 124–126.
2. Hayden Herrera, *Frida: A Biography of Frida Kahlo* (New York: Harper & Row Publishers, 1983), p. 405.
3. Frida Kahlo, compiled by Martha Zamora, *The Letters of Frida Kahlo: Cartas Apasionadas* (San Francisco: Chronicle Books, 1995), p. 155.
4. Zamora, p. 126.
5. Diego Rivera, *My Art, My Life: An Autobiography* (Mineola, N.Y.: Dover Publications, Inc., 1991), p.177.

CHAPTER 2. A DIFFICULT START

1. Malka Drucker, *Frida Kahlo* (Albuquerque: University of New Mexico Press, 1995), p. 5.
2. Frida Kahlo, with an introduction by Carlos Fuentes, *The Diary of Frida Kahlo* (New York: Harry Abrams, Inc., 1998), p. 282.
3. Ibid., p. 248.
4. Andrea Kettenmann, *Frida Kahlo: Pain and Passion* (Koln, Germany: Taschen, 2002), p. 7.
5. Hayden Herrera, *Frida Kahlo: The Paintings* (New York: HarperCollins Publishers, 1991), p. 29.
6. Raquel Tibol, Elinor Randall, trans. *Frida Kahlo: An Open Life* (Albuquerque: University of New Mexico Press, 1993), p. 10.
7. Isabel Alcantara and Sandra Egnolf, *Frida Kahlo and Diego Rivera* (New York: Prestel, 1999), p. 9.

8. Ibid.
9. Tibol, p. 39.
10. Kahlo, p. 282.

CHAPTER 3. CHANGED FOREVER

1. Martha Zamora, Marilyn Sode Smith, trans., *Frida Kahlo: The Brush of Anguish* (San Francisco: Chronicle Books, 1990), p. 19.
2. Malka Drucker, *Frida Kahlo* (Albuquerque: University of New Mexico Press, 1995), p. 12.
3. Andrea Kettenmann, *Frida Kahlo: Pain and Passion* (Koln, Germany: Taschen, 2002), p. 20.
4. Jack Rummel, *Frida Kahlo: A Spiritual Biography* (New York: Crossroad Publishing Company, 2000), p. 42.
5. Isabel Alcantara and Sandra Egnolf, *Frida Kahlo and Diego Rivera* (New York: Prestel, 1999), p. 14.
6. Ibid., p. 11.
7. Drucker, p. 15.
8. Hayden Herrera, *Frida Kahlo: The Paintings* (New York: HarperCollins Publishers, 1991), p. 41.
9. Rummel, p. 42.
10. Frida Kahlo, with an introduction by Carlos Fuentes, *The Diary of Frida Kahlo* (New York: Harry Abrams, Inc., 1998), p. 21.
11. Drucker, p. 14.
12. Rummel, p. 51.
13. Ibid.
14. Norma Broude and Mary D. Garrard, eds., *The Expanding Discourse: Feminism and Art History* (New York: IconEditions, 1992), pp. 397–398.
15. Diego Rivera, *My Art, My Life: An Autobiography* (Mineola, N.Y.: Dover Publications, Inc., 1991), p. 75.

16. Raquel Tibol, Elinor Randall, trans. *Frida Kahlo: An Open Life* (Albuquerque: University of New Mexico Press, 1993), p. 43.

CHAPTER 4. BEGINNING AGAIN

1. Alejandro Arias, *Frida Kahlo and Tina Modotti* (London: Whitechapel Art Gallery, 1982), p. 39.
2. Isabel Alcantara and Sandra Egnolf, *Frida Kahlo and Diego Rivera* (New York: Prestel, 1999), p. 18.
3. Raquel Tibol, Elinor Randall, trans. *Frida Kahlo: An Open Life* (Albuquerque: University of New Mexico Press, 1993), p. 43.
4. Hayden Herrera, *Frida: A Biography of Frida Kahlo* (New York: Harper & Row Publishers, 1983), p. 53.
5. Frida Kahlo, compiled by Martha Zamora, *The Letters of Frida Kahlo: Cartas Apasionadas* (San Francisco: Chronicle Books, 1995), p. 23.
6. Jack Rummel, *Frida Kahlo: A Spiritual Biography* (New York: Crossroad Publishing Company, 2000), p. 56.
7. Kahlo, p. 22.
8. Herrera, p. 56.
9. Arias, p. 39.
10. Rummel, p. 55.
11. Erika Billeter, *The Blue House: The World of Frida Kahlo* (Seattle: University of Washington Press, in association with the Museum of Fine Arts, Houston, 1993), p. 11.
12. Kahlo, p. 33.
13. Ibid., p. 29.
14. Ibid., p. 31.
15. Diego Rivera, *My Art, My Life: An Autobiography* (Mineola, N.Y.: Dover Publications, Inc., 1991), p. 67.
16. Ibid., p. 102.
17. Ibid., pp. 102–103.

18. Hayden Herrera, *Frida Kahlo: The Paintings* (New York: HarperCollins Publishers, 1991), p. 48.

19. Martha Zamora, Marilyn Sode Smith, trans., *Frida Kahlo: The Brush of Anguish* (San Francisco: Chronicle Books, 1990), p. 40.

20. Ibid., p. 37.

21. Herrera, Frida: *A Biography of Frida Kahlo*, p. 95.

22. Ibid., p. 96

23. Norma Broude and Mary D. Garrard, eds., *The Expanding Discourse: Feminism and Art History* (New York: IconEditions, 1992), p. 399.

CHAPTER 5. LIFE IN LOVE

1. Isabel Alcantara and Sandra Egnolf, *Frida Kahlo and Diego Rivera* (New York: Prestel, 1999), p. 34.

2. Martha Zamora, Marilyn Sode Smith, trans., *Frida Kahlo: The Brush of Anguish* (San Francisco: Chronicle Books, 1990), p. 80.

3. Hayden Herrera, *Frida: A Biography of Frida Kahlo* (New York: Harper & Row Publishers, 1983), p. 110.

4. Ibid., p. 105.

5. Ibid., p. 102.

6. Diego Rivera, *My Art, My Life: An Autobiography* (Mineola, N.Y.: Dover Publications, Inc., 1991), p. 105.

7. Frida Kahlo, compiled by Martha Zamora, *The Letters of Frida Kahlo: Cartas Apasionadas* (San Francisco: Chronicle Books, 1995), p. 15.

8. Edward Weston, *The Daybooks of Edward Weston, Book II* (New York: Horizon Press, 1961), p. 198.

9. Jack Rummel, *Frida Kahlo: A Spiritual Biography* (New York: Crossroad Publishing Company, 2000), p. 83.

10. Kahlo, p. 41.

11. Ibid., p. 40.

12. Rummel, p. 85.
13. Norma Broude and Mary D. Garrard, eds., *The Expanding Discourse: Feminism and Art History* (New York: IconEditions, 1992), p. 403.
14. Kahlo, p. 42.
15. Ibid., p. 43.
16. Ibid.

CHAPTER 6. DIARY ON CANVAS

1. Bertram D. Wolfe, *The Fabulous Life of Diego Rivera* (New York: Stein and Day Publishers, 1984), p. 297.
2. Diego Rivera, *My Art, My Life: An Autobiography* (Mineola, N.Y.: Dover Publications, Inc., 1991), p. 109.
3. Wolfe, p. 301.
4. Malka Drucker, *Frida Kahlo* (Albuquerque: University of New Mexico Press, 1995), pp. 57–59.
5. Rivera, pp. 111–112.
6. Ibid., p. 111.
7. Wolfe, p. 309.
8. Ibid.
9. Rivera, p. 124.
10. Andrea Kettenmann, *Frida Kahlo: Pain and Passion* (Koln, Germany: Taschen, 2002), p. 36.
11. Wolfe, p. 314.
12. Hayden Herrera, *Frida: A Biography of Frida Kahlo* (New York: Harper & Row Publishers, 1983), p. 135.
13. Ibid.

CHAPTER 7. GOING HOME

1. Hayden Herrera, *Frida: A Biography of Frida Kahlo* (New York: Harper & Row Publishers, 1983), p. 162.
2. Bertram D. Wolfe, *The Fabulous Life of Diego Rivera* (New York: Stein and Day Publishers, 1984), p. 324.

3. Diego Rivera, *My Art, My Life: An Autobiography* (Mineola, N.Y.: Dover Publications, Inc., 1991), p. 126.
4. Hayden Herrera, *Frida Kahlo: The Paintings* (New York: HarperCollins Publishers, 1991), p. 105.
5. Frida Kahlo, compiled by Martha Zamora, *The Letters of Frida Kahlo: Cartas Apasionadas* (San Francisco: Chronicle Books, 1995), p. 61.
6. Andrea Kettenmann, *Frida Kahlo: Pain and Passion* (Koln, Germany: Taschen, 2002), p. 39.

CHAPTER 8. TORN APART

1. Hayden Herrera, *Frida Kahlo: The Paintings* (New York: HarperCollins Publishers, 1991), pp. 57–58.
2. Ibid., p. 75.
3. Hayden Herrera, *Frida: A Biography of Frida Kahlo* (New York: Harper & Row Publishers, 1983), p. 226.
4. Whitney Chadwick, *Women Artists and the Surrealist Movement* (Boston: Little, Brown and Company, 1985), p. 87.
5. Herrera, *Frida: A Biography of Frida Kahlo*, p. 266.
6. Alejandro Arias, *Frida Kahlo and Tina Modotti* (London: Whitechapel Art Gallery, 1982), p. 36.
7. Ibid.
8. Jack Rummel, *Frida Kahlo: A Spiritual Biography* (New York: Crossroad Publishing Company, 2000), p. 120.
9. Andrea Kettenmann, *Frida Kahlo: Pain and Passion* (Koln, Germany: Taschen, 2002), p. 45.
10. Herrera, *Frida: A Biography of Frida Kahlo*, p. 238.
11. Rummel, p. 126.
12. Diego Rivera, *My Art, My Life: An Autobiography* (Mineola, N.Y.: Dover Publications, Inc., 1991), p. 138.
13. Herrera, *Frida: A Biography of Frida Kahlo*, pp. 245–246.
14. Rivera, p. 138.

15. Herrera, *Frida: A Biography of Frida Kahlo*, pp. 272–273.
16. Herrera, *Frida Kahlo: The Paintings*, pp. 135–138.

CHAPTER 9. COMING TO TERMS

1. Hayden Herrera, *Frida: A Biography of Frida Kahlo* (New York: Harper & Row Publishers, 1983), p. 294.
2. Jack Rummel, *Frida Kahlo: A Spiritual Biography* (New York: Crossroad Publishing Company, 2000), pp. 133–134.
3. Diego Rivera, *My Art, My Life: An Autobiography* (Mineola, N.Y.: Dover Publications, Inc., 1991), pp. 149–150.
4. Ibid., p. 150.
5. Andrea Kettenmann, *Frida Kahlo: Pain and Passion* (Koln, Germany: Taschen, 2002), p. 61.
6. Frida Kahlo, compiled by Martha Zamora, *The Letters of Frida Kahlo: Cartas Apasionadas* (San Francisco: Chronicle Books, 1995), pp. 111–112.
7. Herrera, p. 281.
8. Ibid., p. 307.
9. Kahlo, p. 113.
10. Guadalupe Rivera and Marie-Pierre Colle, Kenneth Krabbenhoft, trans., *Frida's Fiestas: Recipes and Reminiscences of Life with Frida Kahlo* (New York: Clarkson Potter Publishers, 1994), p. 203.
11. Ibid., p. 205.
12. Ibid., p. 98.
13. Ibid.
14. Herrera, p. 316.
15. Ibid., p. 330.
16. Raquel Tibol, Elinor Randall, trans. *Frida Kahlo: An Open Life* (Albuquerque: University of New Mexico Press, 1993), p. 180.
17. Malka Drucker, *Frida Kahlo* (Albuquerque: University of New Mexico Press, 1995), pp. 116–117.

18. Jack Rummel, *Frida Kahlo: A Spiritual Biography* (New York: Crossroad Publishing Company, 2000), p. 152.
19. Herrera, p. 331.
20. Ibid., p. 344.
21. Kahlo, p. 121.
22. Herrera, p. 353.
23. Frida Kahlo, with an introduction by Carlos Fuentes, *The Diary of Frida Kahlo* (New York: Harry Abrams, Inc., 1998), p. 252.

CHAPTER 10. A LIFE REMEMBERED

1. Frida Kahlo, with an introduction by Carlos Fuentes, *The Diary of Frida Kahlo* (New York: Harry Abrams, Inc., 1998), p. 252.
2. Isabel Alcantara and Sandra Egnolf, *Frida Kahlo and Diego Rivera* (New York: Prestel, 1999), p. 105.
3. Kahlo, p. 277.
4. Ibid., p. 274.
5. Diego Rivera, *My Art, My Life: An Autobiography* (Mineola, N.Y.: Dover Publications, Inc., 1991), p. 178.
6. Kahlo, p. 278.
7. Hayden Herrera, *Frida: A Biography of Frida Kahlo* (New York: Harper & Row Publishers, 1983), p. 427.
8. Ibid., p. 403.
9. Rivera, p. 178.
10. Ibid., p. 179.
11. Erika Billeter, *The Blue House: The World of Frida Kahlo* (Seattle: University of Washington Press in association with the Museum of Fine Arts, Houston, 1993), p.10.
12. Malka Drucker, *Frida Kahlo: Torment and Triumph in Her Life and Art* (New York: Bantam Books, 1991), p. xi.

Further Reading

Drucker, Malka. *Frida Kahlo*. Albuquerque: University of New Mexico Press, 1995.

Frazier, Nancy. *Frida Kahlo: Mysterious Painter*. Woodbridge, Conn.: Blackbirch Press, 1992.

Lewis, Elizabeth. *Mexican Art and Culture*. Chicago: Raintree, 2004.

Morrison, John. *Frida Kahlo*. Bromall, Pa.: Chelsea House, 2002.

Zamora, Martha, and Marilyn Sode Smith, trans. *Frida Kahlo: The Brush of Anguish*. San Francisco: Chronicle Books, 1990.

INTERNET ADDRESSES

Frida Kahlo and Contemporary Thoughts
<http://www.fridakahlo.it>

The Frida Kahlo Museum
<http://www.mexconnect.com/mex_/travel/grandall/grfridamuseo.html>

Index

Page numbers for photographs are in **boldface** type.